1%
MORE

THE HIDDEN FORCE TO CREATING EXTRAORDINARY RESULTS IN LIFE AND BUSINESS!

Leonard D. DeCarmine

Paperback ISBN: 978-1-953806-98-7
eBook ISBN: 978-1-953806-99-4
Library of Congress Control Number: 2022905827

Front and Back Cover Design: Leonard D. DeCarmine
Proofreading: Valerie Sebestyen
Interior design: Amit Dey
Published by Spotlight Publishing – https://Spotlightpublishing.pro

Contact: Len DeCarmine
https://ExtraordinaryBeingMovement.com

THE HIDDEN FORCE TO CREATING EXTRAORDINARY RESULTS IN LIFE AND BUSINESS!

Leonard D. DeCarmine

Goodyear, AZ

FOREWORD

BY ROBERT W. JONES

*I*t's always an interesting question when I'm asked what makes greatness. As an Entrepreneur, Investor, Event Host, Speaker, and Master Connector, I get asked this question often. In fact, I don't know how many times I've been asked this question. I hear people say, "Is there a secret ingredient?" "Is there a special recipe?" or "Is it passion?" or "Is it obsession?" What is it that one thing that takes the most ordinary of people and makes them into that hidden force, a "something" so extraordinary that their business, character, or thoughts become that world-class 1% difference?

I think about this a lot, because, in fact, it's a good question. It's a question that's not easily answered, and it's a question that may have as many answers as those who asked the questions in the first place. It's not always about just the strategy, the planning, the building, the designing, or even the service. Sometimes it's something that's much more insignificant yet creates the extraordinary that causes people to wonder, "What is it about that person that makes them so special?" So much so that people are willing to give their time their money and make dramatic changes for them.

I recall the first time that Len and I were able to sit down and chat about greatness. We knew within the first few moments that we were connected. It wasn't so much that we had walked the same path, or learned the same lessons, it was that we didn't. What we did though was align on the subject that mattered most, greatness. We both were on a journey to find the hidden force that resides within us all and help each other and others with their journey too.

And that's what this book is about. It's about what it is that creates greatness. It's not just about the ideas, the strategies, the planning, the thoughts, etc. And yes, it is all those things, but really what it gets down to is how a person can increase for themselves a 1% continually, to strive every moment where that 1% becomes "their" 1%, the truest of gifts that any person can give to the world, the ability to tap into that "hidden force."

For this book, I thought about Len. He is a visionary and, in many ways, expresses his own version of that 1% difference. Not just to the exposure, the credibility, the revenue, the profit, but with respect to the moment. With Len, every individual, whether male, or female, black or white, believer or not, and everything in between, greatness matters. Len is that mindful space between the sound of words that creates the needed respite of time for everyone to take their first step, next step, and every step of their own 1% journey.

As the Founder and Owner of one of the largest entrepreneurial networking and training organizations in the world, I have found Len DeCarmine a gifted, heart-centered trainer, influencer, coach, and friend. Although, at least at this point, he may not be a household name, of those who we think about in the greatness space, he will be. And it's my privilege to be a part of his journey, one that I hope will shine for years to come.

As our lives are being disrupted and the challenges become greater and faster, Len helps entrepreneurs, business owners, and influencers take the time to slow down, breathe deeply, and build a foundation that lasts a lifetime. He doesn't stop with skills, he connects people, he provides resources, and his coaching is unapologetic and transformative. He listens to the inner feelings of his clients and helps them find a life of happiness, joy, and prosperity without apology.

For this book, *1 % More - The Hidden Force to Creating Extraordinary Results in Life and Business,* Len has brought together some of the world's leaders in what I call thought technology, those who are willing to open themselves to help others, help develop their hearts and minds, to create a new beginning. So, bring your empty cup to "class." Let's enjoy this journey with Len, me, and the other authors of this book. All who have and will share their story with other entrepreneurs, business owners, and Influencers seeking their own personal freedom. Now you, too can be inspired to increase your very own universe 1% at a time, infinitely.

DEDICATION

*I am dedicating this book to all those who believed in me
when I struggled to believe in myself.*

*Thank you to the contributors, podcast guests,
and the people who have come into my life over the years.
If it weren't for the experiences we shared, big and small,
I would not be here today!*

*A special thank you to my friends and family who stood by
my side throughout the years, especially my mother.
I would not be able to continue my journey without her
love and support.*

- Thank you!

Epigraph

"The difference between ordinary and extraordinary is that little extra."

- *Jimmy Johnson*

PREFACE

In the summer of 2018, looking to enhance my coaching skills, I joined a Meetup group on Neuro-Linguistic Programming (otherwise known as NLP). NLP is an approach that looks at how we process our experiences through our senses, the ways we communicate both verbally and non-verbally, and how we respond to situations in our lives. It's excellent training for anyone, no matter if their interest level is professional or casual.

The group met in an office complex meeting room every Wednesday night from 7-8 pm. Usually there were about a dozen of us sitting around a large conference table. The room always lacked enough chairs, so many times we had to wheel them in from other offices and sit packed tightly together. We didn't mind; we all believed in the benefits of Neuro-Linguistic Programming and the power behind it, so we were eager to learn!

The students in the room ranged from all ages and backgrounds, from life coaches, salespeople, and real estate agents to curious people just looking for ways to better themselves. One of the members of the group leaders was Christopher Shiver, a young, well-spoken man full of confidence. At the time, Chris was working as an intern and student for the NLP Coaching & Skills Training Institute. Chris is trained as an NLP Master Practitioner and Trainer, teaching and leading many Wednesday night classes. He was charming and seemed always to be grabbing the attention of the women in the room.

There also, I met Fred Martinez. Fred had contagious energy as he often shared stories about his experiences as an athlete performing Olympic-style weightlifting, dating, and relationships. He is outgoing, charismatic, and a great conversationalist. Fred is also the author of the book "Financial Game Plan For Your Dollars and Cents," where he shares his techniques and strategies to become debt-free and make better financial decisions.

After class, Fred, Chris, and I would have chats about NLP, dating, and relationships. Soon our friendship grew outside of class. We periodically got together for lunch and continued our talks for hours. Before long, we realized that each of us was on the same path, a path moving toward change, growth, and finding healthy relationships. It occurred to me that we had something worth sharing with others, and I approached both of them about the potential of creating a podcast to talk about our ideas and opinions on life, relationships, growth, and change, all of the things we were already talking about.

They were excited about this idea, and it didn't take us long to organize and plan our first show. What we needed next was a title. We knew each of us was on a journey to find love, release the past, and build a life of freedom and abundance – and after tossing around various names that encompassed our vision, the ***Extraordinary Being Movement*** was born!

What is the ***Extraordinary Being Movement?***

The ***Extraordinary Being Movement*** holds the idea that we are all extraordinary in our own ways, that each of us has unique gifts, traits, and talents. For our podcast, we seek out people who exemplify this idea. We interview people worldwide who are no longer sitting on the sidelines but are examples of the ***"anything is possible"*** mentality. They share their failures and successes, strategies and techniques on developing relationships, business, spirituality, health, and wealth.

Their stories highlight how others can improve their lives, regardless of background, financial status, or past mistakes. Sadly, many people cannot see beyond their roadblocks, challenges, and memories of the past to be able to move forward. They are playing small in their lives, believing that real change is not possible for them. They have no clear vision of the present, let alone the future. The gifts they have been given are now masked, hidden, or forgotten.

The *Extraordinary Being Movement* is meant to help change that. As a movement and a community, we can show people how to change, develop, and grow. More importantly, we can help you to create change, and find ways to uncover your hidden gifts. Through sharing stories, coaching, and training, the *Extraordinary Being Movement* will guide you in moving forward to discover or rediscover the hidden force within you.

Remember, everything starts with *You*!

Our vision is to create *"A global movement to empower people in personal growth and achievement"* and a community that thrives globally to *Inspire, Influence,* and *Motivate* people to take action, create change, and achieve success. *To become global leaders!*

We do this through our coaching and training to provide clarity and purpose. To create a stronger you, establish healthy relationships, live a life you love, be fulfilled, and most of all feel valued.

As a collective group of business professionals, leaders, and coaches…

Our Movement is about taking a stand for YOU!

We are here to help you gain the knowledge and resources you need to be ready to make that first step, and we are here to support you in your efforts to reach your dreams.

We know you are tired of...

- *Struggling*
- *Being blocked*
- *Dealing with fear and uncertainty*
- *Feeling lost in the world*
- *Not reaching your dreams*

So, let's end the excuses. No more putting blame elsewhere. Accept responsibility and begin to take action, develop ownership and accountability. Create your own set of rules, make an unapologetic commitment to your success, and reawaken your soul!

Join us and be a part of the ***Extraordinary Being Movement*** as we help you break down the walls, stop the consistent mind chatter, and open up your eyes and heart to the unlimited possibilities which await you.

INTRODUCTION

*T*oday's world has changed a lot from even just a few years ago, from how we live, to how we are supposed to act and what we can say. Our minds are overloaded with information, worry, and stress. Tossed about by other people's opinions, our emotions, and our own poor self-judgment, it's hard to make sense of it all and to get ahead in life. Most of us are focused on day-to-day survival, just trying to pay the bills, taking care of our families, and protecting ourselves from things we cannot see, touch, or feel.

It's hard to think in a world that is constantly filled with so much noise. Finding a quiet space to reflect on our own needs and self-care feels nearly impossible at times. We fall into the abyss of everyday life and routines, moving through our days like zombies, living for the weekends and trying to find ways of escape, only to start it all over again on Monday.

This way of living needs to stop!

We have been placed in this world for more than just going through the motions. Our lives are precious, irreplaceable, and one of a kind, yet we don't appreciate what we have been given. We are reckless in our decisions and choices. We damage our minds, body, and souls with harmful substances and thoughts, devaluing our self-worth and abilities when really, we should be living with energy, excitement, and passion!

No more.

You need to begin taking a stand for who you are. Start reflecting on your behaviors, on your current way of interacting with yourself, your friends, family, and co-workers. Take a step back and view life from a different angle. Listen to what you are actually communicating to yourself and to others. You can start to live when you…

- *Stop winging life!*
- *Stop letting life control you!*
- *Stop playing small!*
- *Stop being a victim!*
- *Stop creating false stories!*
- *Stop letting your emotions control you!*
- *Stop thinking negatively!*

You need to start making better choices and learn how to be more resourceful.

In this book, you will hear from many passionate coaches, business professionals, health experts, personal development specialists, and others. They will share their personal stories, techniques, simple strategies, and solutions for dealing with the issues you are facing right now! They offer tools that you can use to harness the hidden force, just like others are doing to make their lives extraordinary!

You will learn how to step away from just getting by day to day to living a fulfilled life with purpose and intention. How do I know? Well, there was a time in my life when I was the nerdy overweight kid in school. Shy and awkward, I kept to myself a lot. I wore superhero shirts and yellow sweatpants and because I had to repeat the second grade due to constantly being sick with strep throat, I was always the oldest kid in class. I was picked on for being socially and athletically inept and for collecting comic books and was called Len-NERD throughout most of my school years.

Most of the time, I felt alone and kept to myself, watching cartoons and creating action scenes with my GI Joe toys just to escape my reality of loneliness. Nothing really improved for me as I aged. By my teenage years, I was still the nerdy kid but spent even more time reading comic books, drawing superheroes, and being alone. I felt depressed, confused, and angry. I told myself over and over that I wasn't good enough, smart enough, attractive enough. I just felt broken and worthless.

In my late teenage years, my uncle introduced me to personal development. He shared a story of his experience performing a fire walk with Tony Robbins, in California.

The idea of how he had to face mind over matter intrigued me. I learned from his experience that with the right mindset anything is possible. I recognized at the age of sixteen what I did not want for my life, and this introduction to the world of personal development changed my direction forever. My eyes were opened to new choices and resources that became available to me. Instead of following a path to drown my pain in drugs and alcohol, I decided to choose my own adventure in life.

Since then, I have dedicated my life to learning all I can in the realm of personal development and other related fields. I've spent over 25 years exploring this new world...

I have absorbed information like a sponge, through books, CDs, cassettes, training programs, seminars, and workshops. I spend my time reading and training on topics of self-help, psychology, spirituality, sociology, communication, business, sales, marketing, and real estate.

I've devoted my time and energy to learn from the great men and women before me, such as Jim Rohn, Dale Carnegie, Napoleon Hill, Earl Nightingale, Jack Canfield, Louise Hay, Brian Tracy, Steven Covey, Byron Katie, Brené Brown, Robert Kiyosaki, and many others. Over the years, I've invested hundreds of hours and thousands of dollars to grow my knowledge on how to empower myself, to live life with intention and purpose. I've learned from both successes and failures, sometimes needing to re-learn lessons or two along the way, but always treasuring each step of this journey, and continue today to learn as much as I can. Through these efforts, I discovered about achieving just 1% more and how phenomenal the impact of 1% more can be.

The processes and strategies you will learn throughout this book to guide you in achieving that 1% more which is focused on four core pillars: *Awareness, Growth, Action,* and *Impact.*

AWARENESS, GROWTH, ACTION, AND IMPACT:
THE 4 CORE PILLARS OF PERSONAL TRANSFORMATION

Awareness - Understanding Yourself and the World Around You - Our world is complex. Even just day-to-day living has gotten complicated. Overwhelmed, we have lost our self-awareness, instead of getting lost in our phones, mindlessly binge-watching television shows, and waiting for the latest social media posts to pop up.

The ***Extraordinary Being Movement*** will help you to emerge from this muddle. We will help you discover yourself and develop a clear sense of who you are. With improved vision, you'll be able to make a plan to further your development and find your way to a greater sense of purpose and meaning. With awareness, you can take back your life, create unstoppable confidence, and open your eyes to wonderment.

Growth - Discovering Your Unlimited Possibilities - Personal growth is a lifelong process of learning, with unlimited possibilities. Successful people understand how critical it is to keep obtaining more knowledge and new skills. They endlessly push themselves outside of their comfort zones to keep unlocking even more of their inner, untapped potential. We want you to explore, push just a little bit further, and discover the wonders hidden inside of you.

Action - Propel Yourself to Success - Awareness provides us the wisdom to understand and growth gives us new resources, but action is what creates change and sets us in motion to achieve results. Here is where many of us fall short, spending our time being busy but not creating any actual outcomes. The ***Extraordinary Being Movement*** will coach you on how to be accountable to yourself and others, utilize your time more effectively, and take responsibility for your choices in the process.

Impact - Bringing the Past and Future Together as One - Life is about learning from the past, living in the present, and building for the future. Imagine what it would be like to let go of all the "stuff" that has been holding you back all these years! All of the pain, sorrow and regret now provide forgiveness and empowerment. You can create intentional results. What would that look like? How would it feel? Who would you become?

Impact is the synergy you create from leveraging the power of *Awareness, Growth,* and *Action*. It is the result of the transformation that YOU create which causes significant changes in your life, changes that are meaningful and purposeful. Impact gives you the freedom to shape your life and make extraordinary changes, not only in your life but also in the lives of others.

Let's take a moment and look at your life right now. Think about it. You made it this far, right? But is it where you want to be? Does it resonate within your soul? We all get caught in a cycle. A cycle of doing the same thing over and over again. Imagine yourself as a hamster running on a wheel. You keep running around as fast as you can, thinking that your life is getting somewhere, yet it doesn't.

Eventually, exhausted, you feel burned out and hopeless. You can continue doing what you have always been doing, day in and day out until you make that conscious decision to stop.

To get off that wheel to nowhere, I decided to make a choice, a choice to take responsibility and do the work necessary to transform - certainly, in my case, it took serious focus and a determination to examine these pillars of my life.

Take a step back and look at how most people think and act in life. Many people are winging it. They live in ignorance and fear of the unknown. They lack awareness of the impact of their choices and don't see the harm they are doing to themselves and others. They are blind to the hidden and unknown conditions that show up in their lives from repressed or subconscious feelings or behaviors and attitudes from past childhood experiences. Instead of facing them, they continue their lives being *"okay"* or *"fine"* but never take responsibility for how they think, act, and behave.

Their lives stay stagnant with no new development or growth. They are always wondering, *Why me? What can't I get ahead in life? Why do bad things always happen to me?* Eventually, they become frustrated and angry and continue their lives as if they have a dark cloud lingering over their head.

Not until they are faced with an ultimatum, do they finally take action. Now, their backs are against the wall. Survival mode has been activated, and they become stressed, emotional, and resentful of the situation they caused but still everyone else is at fault. At this point, many people are in over their heads. The problem has already worsened, continuing a cycle some people have faced for years.

If you think about these three ways, living in the unknown, living in stagnation, and being forced into an ultimatum, what is the common element? You are. You're the center of it all. There is only so much time in our lives, you only have so much energy to give. According to the Wealth Research Group, 98% of people die without fulfilling their dreams. Why should you be part of this statistic? It takes the same amount of energy to live your life under a dark cloud of negativity as it does living your life in the light of positivity.

THE UNKNOWNS CAUSE STAGNATION UNTIL YOU ARE FACED
WITH AN ULTIMATUM

But for you, there is hope! You can create change, but only if you are ready to take action to end the cycle and get off that wheel. I know it may be a bit intimidating, but you won't be alone.

My Discovery

Step one of my discovery was realizing that I don't have to live in a world of the unknown. I began by building self-awareness by asking better questions. Instead of asking *"Why me?"* which limited my answers and focused on all the negativity in my life, I began asking, *"What can I do differently?"* This question opened up new possibilities to explore. It allowed me to think differently and view the situation from a different perspective.

I also asked people how I showed up to them, what they liked, and did not like about me. Asking for this type of feedback is sometimes hard to swallow, but I knew if I wanted to change, I had to grow my awareness. The power of self-awareness comes from accepting who you are, not just the identity you project, but all of your external and internal traits. Understanding yourself helps you become a better decision-maker, provides you clarity, and increases your confidence and self-esteem.

To deal with stagnation in my life, I needed to start taking chances. Regardless of fear, I fought through my discomfort by moving outside my comfort zone. I built my confidence by educating myself, meeting new people, and experiencing new situations. I was able to heighten my awareness and expand my mind.

Instead of waiting for things to happen to me, I took immediate responsibility for my life and took action. I didn't wait for an ultimatum to happen and be forced to have my back against a wall. I addressed damaged relationships and broken agreements and accepted ownership over what I was responsible for in the situation. I started to develop a system and strategies to hold me accountable, achieve my goals, and build upon better habits.

All three of these had an extraordinary impact on my life. I began to see more choices and opportunities in front of me. Relationships began to heal. Agreements were restored. I realized that there was so much more hidden inside me than I could have ever imagined.

Personal Transformation:
Powerful Questions, Systems + Strategies, Stretch Zone

ABOUT THIS BOOK

This book is divided into four sections: *Awareness, Growth, Action,* and *Impact.* These four concepts represent the *Extraordinary Being Movement's* pillars to transformation. In each section, carefully selected authors will expand upon these pillars and share their insights, stories, strategies, as well as systems to help further you in life and business. The authors in the book were chosen based upon their unique talents, areas of interest, and professionalism. They are all excited to be part of your journey!

The chapters will guide you deeper into the lessons and strategies associated with each pillar. Many chapters will provide activities and questions to help reinforce your knowledge to take immediate action. Please take your time reading the book, take notes, and apply what you have learned because this is the first step toward transformation!

YOUR JOURNEY BEGINS WITH YOU!

You have the power right now to begin creating a new version of you, a version that is purposeful, intentional, deliberate, and meaningful. You have the power to take back control of your life in areas that are not working and begin improving them immediately by observing the issues from a different perspective and opening your heart and soul to new opportunities. Ask yourself the following questions as you read through this book…

- *What area of my life would I like to improve today?*

- *What would that change look and feel like?*
- *What story would I like to live and leave as a legacy?*
- *What would it be like if I could achieve more with less?*
- *What ways can I make these strategies work best for my life?*

As you start asking yourself these questions, more opportunities and resources will become available to you. The tools presented in this book will help you build a foundation for success.

Over the years, I have used these tools to create positive changes for myself. My confidence grew every time I discovered a new unknown in my life. I took action to address the unknown and design an approach to make the change to create a new habit for success. A new world began to open up for me. I took greater responsibility for my actions, became accountable for what I say and do, and hold myself to a higher level of integrity. It has become easier for me to hold my head up and walk with confidence.

That is why I am certain that this book will help you develop the power to invent new possibilities. As coaches, everyone who contributed to this book wants you to be inspired to take action, create change, and feel motivated for success. Success doesn't happen overnight but if you are committed, willing to learn, and have the courage to take action, then you have the power to do that *1% More* to unlock the hidden force within you.

If you know someone else who is struggling, looking for guidance, or needs clearer insight, please share with them so they too can benefit in harnessing the power of *1 % More - The Hidden Force to Creating Extraordinary Results in Life and Business!*

Ready? Let's begin…

Table Of Contents

Foreword - Robert W. Jones . . . . *v*

Dedication. . . . . *ix*

Epigraph . . . . *xi*

Preface . . . . *xiii*

Introduction - ONE PERCENT MORE . . . . *xvii*

The Pillars: AWARENESS / GROWTH / ACTION / IMPACT. . . *xx*

About This Book. . . . . *xxvii*

Pillar One - AWARENESS. *1*

Chapter 1: Understanding Yourself and the World
Around You 3

Chapter 2: Self Discovery, The Pathway to Change. 5

Chapter 3: Creating Self Awareness 13

Chapter 4: Living life with Intention 21

Chapter 5: The Unspoken Truth: Be The Real You
By Teresa Porter 25

Chapter 6: Self-Alignment Coaching
By Agne Paceviciute 33

Chapter 7: Stop Chasing Joy. Begin Living In Wonder!
By Dr. Karthik Ramanan. 41

Chapter 8: Mindset Will Lead You To Your Purpose
    By Allison Noelle Megherian 49

Chapter 9: How I Learned Pure F**kin' Magic

    By Nadine Sabulsky 55

Pillar Two - Growth *63*

Chapter 10: The Five Areas of Growth. 65

Chapter 11: Be Comfortable In Being Uncomfortable 71

Chapter 12: The Cycle of Integrity 77

Chapter 13: The Seed of Greatness
    By Alexander Richmond. 85

Chapter 14: Life Activated
    By Alicia Thorp. 91

Chapter 15: Multi-Dimensional Reality
    By Teresa Martell 97

Chapter 16: The Epiphany
    By Craig Darling. 103

Chapter 17: The Art of Being You
    By Corryn Kivett. 109

Chapter 18: The Healing Power of Story
    By Becky Norwood. 117

Chapter 19: Growing Beyond Limitations
    By Christopher Shiver. 127

Chapter 20: Partnership Can Take the Form of Many Things
    By Robert W. Jones 133

Chapter 21: What Does Being a Warrior Mean to You?
    By Frederick Martinez 139

Chapter 22: Your Style Creates Your Life – There's
Just No Way Around It   By Stan Cole 147

Pillar Three - Action *155*

Chapter 23: Lights, Camera, Action! 157

Chapter 24: Creating a System that Works. 161

Chapter 25: Leveling Up Your Goals. 167

Chapter 26: Breaking Bad, Creating New Habits that Last 173

Chapter 27: Create and Live Free
By Jeremy Nicolaides 181

Chapter 28: Please Place Your Mask Over Your Own Mouth and
Nose Before Assisting   By Alexis Braunfeld 189

Chapter 29: Choosing Happiness
By Carrie Vee (Verrocchio) .197

Chapter 30: What Are My Five Love Highlights?
By Nicole Harvick. 215

Chapter 31: Reveal Your Rockstar
By Darryn Yates 223

Chapter 32: Winner's Mindset: On and Off the Field
By Danielle Fagan. 231

Chapter 33: Position of Control – Mastering the Zorro Circle
By David Medansky 239

Chapter 34: Five Golden Rules of Sales to Get People to Take
Action   By Mike Lamothe. .247

Chapter 35: Success or Failure – The Choice is Yours
By Tom Loegering and TJ Loegering. 253

Pillar Four - Impact *263*

Chapter 36: Four Futures, One Choice 265

Chapter 37: The Hidden Force Within 269

Chapter 38: The Power of One Percent 273

Summary – The One Percent More Path *275*

PILLAR ONE

AWARENESS

CHAPTER 1

UNDERSTANDING YOURSELF AND THE WORLD AROUND YOU!

*It's impossible to map out a route to your destination
if you don't know where you are starting from.*

— Suze Orman

As a kid, I loved going to the mall and checking out the giant kiosk in the middle of the walkway. I would start at the big circle stating, *"You Are Here,"* then intensely examine the map, looking for my favorite place, the toy store. Once located, I would calculate the fastest route to get there. I knew if I went five shops down, made a left, and passed Macy's Department Store, I would find my destination, my place of happiness!

What excitement I felt when I got there like I had made it to heaven! As I walked in, I could smell the distinctive scent of new toys awaiting me. At the entrance, the latest remote-control cars, bikes, superheroes, video games, robots, and dolls were neatly displayed. As I swiftly passed these and traveled deeper into the store, I could see everything laid out in front of me in well-kept rows, each with a brightly colored sign telling me where I was and where I needed to go. I dragged my mom by the hand, pulling her as fast as I could to my favorite aisle.

Here in the row labeled *"Action Figures"* is where I would find amazing toys, like GI Joe, Marvel Superheroes, He-Man, and the Teenage Mutant Ninja Turtles, to name a few.

As I've grown older, I've realized that life is not as simple as looking at a map on a mall kiosk, finding the ***"You Are Here"*** dot, and seeing the pathway laid out in front of me to reach my destination. Instead, life allows us to create our own maps and routes to achieve our goals and attain our happiness however that looks to you or me.

Right now, here is where you need to be; this is your starting point no matter your current circumstances, good or bad. You are here for a reason, call it fate, the universe, or divine intervention. Sometimes we don't know why things in life happen, but at this moment, it means they brought you here with me.

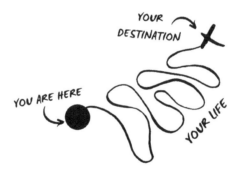

A clear pathway to success and a life of happiness needs a clear starting and ending point. Mapping out our path isn't easy; it takes us through twists and turns, unexpected terrain, and mountains to climb. Even though the course isn't perfect or pretty, we are gifted with the power of choice, a choice to stay on the path of least resistance or to carve out our own. It's like the style of a *Choose Your Own Adventure* book. While this can be exciting and adventurous, it can also be confusing and complex.

So, where do you begin?

CHAPTER 2

SELF-DISCOVERY, THE PATHWAY TO CHANGE!

*"Everyone thinks of changing the world,
but no one thinks of changing himself."*

— *Leo Tolstoy*

Let's begin to reflect on our lives and gain an understanding of what is *"Working"* and what is *"Not Working."* This technique will allow you to come face to face with areas that may need improvement. It will provide insight into various parts of your life, such as career, health, finances, relationships, and even your romantic life.

PERSONAL INVENTORY CHECKLIST

WORKING	NOT WORKING

I would like you first to take out a piece of paper or use your tablet and draw two columns and label them *"Working"* and *"Not Working."* Begin to brainstorm items for your two columns; write down the first things that come to mind. Don't worry about what comes out. Just unload it all and come up with at least 8-10 items under each column.

Please don't judge yourself on the items you write down or focus on coming up with solutions at this point. Just clear your mind and release all the things that may be weighing you down. You may see an unbalanced column with more on the *"Not Working"* side compared to the *"Working"* side, and that's okay. It just means that you have areas of improvement and opportunity; don't feel overwhelmed or worried. We all have areas that can use improvement.

You've got 8-10 items on your list, now what?

It's time to divide and conquer! Review your *"Not Working"* list and brainstorm potential solutions to them. I recommend you start with one item in your *"Not Working"* column to focus on. For myself, I decided to pick "Health" as the place to start and figure out how I could get the most out of it. My health and fitness are important enough to me to get up early and go to the gym. I have a workout routine in place and dedicate an hour to getting it done. Even though I am consistent, though, I've realized as I've gotten older that working out by itself isn't enough. At one point, my joints were aching, I felt more fatigued throughout my day, and my recovery time took longer.

Below my list, I wrote out in detail all the specific items which were *"Not Working"* for my health.

- *Not enough sleep*
- *Not seeing the doctor regularly*
- *Not taking my heart medication*
- *Not stretching enough*

- *Not eating right*
- *Not seeing other health professionals, nutritionist, chiropractor*
- *Not having a personal trainer*
- *Not enough energy*

PERSONAL INVENTORY CHECKLIST

AREA TO IMPROVE	NOT WORKING
HEALTH	- NOT ENOUGH SLEEP - NOT SEEING THE DOCTOR REGULARLY - NOT TAKING MY HEART MEDICATION - NOT STRETCHING ENOUGH - NOT EATING RIGHT - NOT SEEING OTHER HEALTH PROFESSIONALS, NUTRITIONIST, CHIROPRACTOR - NOT HAVING A PERSONAL TRAINER FOR MEN OVER 40 - NOT ENOUGH ENERGY

I began visualizing my future and thought about what I would be facing down the road if I continued on this path without making changes. I asked myself the following questions…

- *What would my likely outcome be five, ten, twenty years down the road?*
- *Will I be able to continue this way, or would I fall into other health-related issues?*
- *How would my lack of personal accountability affect others in my life?*

I knew I had to be intentional with my thoughts and actions. I could stay where I was because it had been working *"okay"* so far. But if I genuinely wanted to stay, look, and feel healthy, I needed to start doing more than just working out. I had to commit to a broader definition of health. By figuring out my weaknesses, I could consider my options, decide what changes to make, and create a plan to put those changes into action. That meant I had to become accountable and take ownership of my well-being and health. I had to work on myself and be willing to step outside of my comfort zone to make these changes.

Creating change is not simple; it's scary, hard, and frustrating, and sometimes where we think we should be creating change may not be the best place to start. But change doesn't have to happen all at once, in one big chunk. Taking small actionable steps will get you there just as fast, if not faster; it's about doing *1% More!*

I realized that I wanted to make changes to my life and for me doing *1% More* meant making a promise to myself to approach my health from a different viewpoint. I looked at the individual items on my list and brainstormed solutions and possibilities for my issues, such as:

- *Going to bed earlier*
- *Scheduling routine appointments with my doctor*
- *Updating my medication and taking it regularly*
- *Stretching before workouts*
- *Eating healthier*
- *Finding other health-support professionals, like a nutritionist and chiropractor*
- *Getting a personal trainer*
- *Drinking more water*

PERSONAL INVENTORY CHECKLIST

AREA TO IMPROVE	NEW POSSIBILITES
HEALTH	- GOING TO BED EARLIER - SCHEDULING ROUTINE APPOINTMENTS WITH MY DOCTOR - UPDATED MY MEDICATION AND TAKING IT REGULARLY - STRETCHING BEFORE WORKOUTS - EATING HEALTHIER - FINDING OTHER HEALTH PROFESSIONALS, LIKE A NUTRITIONIST, CHIROPRACTOR - GETTING A PERSONAL TRAINER - DRINKING MORE WATER

Performing this exercise opened my mind to see the bigger picture about my health. Some of the answers I wrote out I liked, others I didn't. I chose the ones I felt were the best options for me. With these, I could focus on my intention of living healthier than I did before.

Eventually, I found that making these small changes began to have a huge impact on my life. When I ate healthier, I had more energy. With more sleep, I was well-rested and started to feel more alive. More importantly, becoming self-aware in just this one small area helped me learn how to be mindful overall, and this was a lesson I have been able to apply in other areas of my life.

This exercise, thinking about what is *"Working"* and what is *"Not Working,"* has helped me make sense of more significant issues and provided me a starting point to solving problems and preparing myself for the changes I needed to make. Sorting through my thoughts and jotting down ideas helped me uncover blind spots in my life.

Let's stop here for a minute so you can answer the following to begin your self-discovery!

What areas do you feel are working for you?

_____

_____

_____

_____

_____

_____

What areas do you feel are not working for you?

_____

_____

_____

_____

_____

_____

Pick one area you would like to work on. What in particular is not working?

_____

_____

_____

_____

_____

_____

What new solutions or possibilities can you create within that area?

_____

_____

_____

_____

_____

_____

What did you uncover? Did you create new solutions and possibilities?

If you answer "yes," I congratulate you. If you feel you are struggling, don't worry. Take your time and keep exploring.

CHAPTER 3

CREATING SELF AWARENESS!

*"Until you make the unconscious conscious,
it will direct your life and you will call it fate."*

— *C.G. Jung*

When it comes to personal growth and self-awareness, you need to understand blind spots. Blind spots are hidden areas in our behaviors and thoughts that we can't see. They may include values, habits, thoughts, feelings, traits, and actions. If you haven't thought about or analyzed your blind spots, you've been missing out on a great opportunity to uncover the hidden boundaries that are holding you back.

These blind spots are typically invisible to us and are not easy to recognize on the conscious level. They stop us from living a fulfilled life, but once discovered increase our level of self-awareness. For example, as children, we develop defense mechanisms to protect us from fear and unpleasant emotions, perhaps from abuse, abandonment, or neglect. As we mature into adults, these defense mechanisms become obstacles that block our transformational growth to live a more fulfilled and happier relationship. Once these blind spots are revealed and addressed, our ability to adapt and change increases dramatically and assists us in moving forward *1% More!*

A blind spot is like the wind. You can't see it, but you certainly feel its effects. Maybe you recognize some of these effects in your own life...

- *No matter who you date, every relationship is just like the last*
- *You always feel "unlucky" in life*
- *People don't see you the way you see yourself*
- *You find yourself asking "why does this always happen to me?"*

To break the unpleasant cycle that blind spots cause, you must recognize them for what they are, an unhealthy pattern. Figuring this out will accelerate your journey to a higher self-awareness, providing you with a deeper level of self-knowledge and understanding than you otherwise would have in your life.

This quote from the late Donald Rumsfeld, a former Secretary of Defense, provides us another view of understanding blind spots:

> *There are known knowns. These are things we know that we know. There are known unknowns. That is to say, there are things that we know we don't know. But there are also unknown unknowns. There are things we don't know we don't know.*

Let me explain further with a long-established framework called *Knowns and Unknowns.* The Greek philosopher Plato credits his mentor Socrates with saying, "I know that I know nothing." In the 13th century, Persian poet and philosopher Ibn Yami developed this idea into a method of thought to explore and categorize people according to their knowledge. More recently, in 1955, psychologists Joseph Luft and Harrington Ingham developed what is known as the *Johari Window* technique. This model is designed to help people better understand and evaluate what they know (think) about themselves in contrast to what other people know (think) about them.

Learning about Knowns and Unknowns has been something we as human beings have been trying to understand for centuries. The framework can help us to understand our approach to knowledge, research, and to exploration. Questions such as…

- *What do we know already? (known knowns)*
- *What do we know about our assumptions? (known unknowns)*
- *What unconscious biases could be driving our decisions? (unknown knowns)*
- *How do we become aware of what we could be exploring? (unknown unknowns)*

Thinking in terms of these questions offers up an opportunity to take a deeper look to see what is possibly missing, taking in all of our knowledge or lack thereof. Blind spots are those aspects of ourselves we don't see, such as preferences, habits, dislikes, and prejudiced thoughts, all of which shape our behaviors. Just because we don't, or can't, see them doesn't mean they are not affecting us. They block our ability to understand ourselves and diminish our effectiveness at living a fulfilled life. They are how others see and describe us through a third-person external perception.

Take a moment and imagine a large circle representing your knowledge. Let's carve out a piece to represent "***What You Know***." This category includes information that you are aware of and understand, like how to read, how to write, how to drive a car, how to take out the trash. It also includes facts, like 'the sky is blue.' These are things that you know.

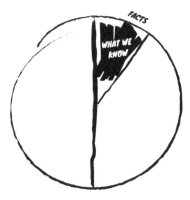

KNOWNS + UNKNOWNS - WHAT WE KNOW - FACTS

Next, we carve out a second area to represent *"What You Know You Don't Know."* These are things that we are aware of but don't exactly understand. For example, you know that it's possible to fly a plane, but you don't know how. You know that water boils when it gets hot, but you might not know the exact temperature required. Usually, these are things you can ask questions about to learn more. You are aware that "I know that I don't know." Here you may need to ask more questions to gain the necessary knowledge.

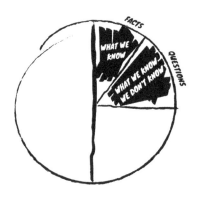

KNOWNS + UNKNOWNS -
WHAT WE KNOW WE DON'T KNOW - QUESTIONS

Let's add a third sliver to the circle that represents *"**What You Don't Know You Know.**"* This may be information or knowledge that lurks in your subconscious and can be considered your intuition. Often it is an unsettled matter that you sense intuitively but are not ready to face openly. For example, you sense something is wrong with your relationship. You know deep inside that it won't work but you haven't yet accepted that it needs to end. You are concealing the truth on a subconscious level because letting it surface–having to face it–is a terrifying thought. You protect yourself by pushing the issue away from your awareness.

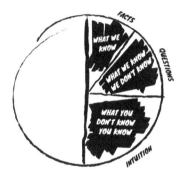

**KNOWNS + UNKNOWNS –
WHAT YOU DON'T KNOW YOU KNOW – INTUITION**

The final and most prominent part of the circle represents the things *"**You Don't Know You Don't Know.**"* This section symbolizes the hidden gaps in your knowledge, gaps you aren't even aware exist in your life. On the simplest level, you may catch yourself saying, *If I had only known* the driver would be two hours late, I wouldn't have rushed to get ready. *If I had only known* that the car I rented was too small for all my luggage, I would have chosen something larger.

On a more complex level, this is where your blind spots hamper you and hold you back from achieving your goals. This is where you may need the assistance of a friend, family member, or coach to see from their view what you can't see about yourself. This feedback will help identify aspects of your hidden personality so you can move forward. Be prepared and keep your mind open to receive constructive criticism and feedback. Remember, exploring your blind spots is necessary if you want to live an extraordinary life.

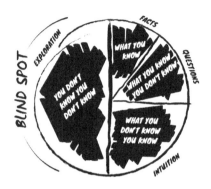

KNOWNS + UNKNOWNS –
YOU DON'T KNOW, YOU DON'T KNOW – EXPLORATION

I will say, going on this journey to discover your blind spots will not be easy. When you start to uncover hidden aspects of yourself, you are likely to feel uncomfortable. No one likes to admit to being flawed, especially in ways they hadn't even thought about before. Uncovering your blind spots can be a complex and delicate process, but it is extremely insightful and a powerful tool for fostering your growth. Understanding yourself better means having more information, and having more information means making smarter decisions and creating better results.

I realized that my life was full of blind spots in almost every area, as a parent, a friend, a co-worker, a lover, a communicator, and a leader. These blind spots were holding me back from reaching and sharing my true potential in all of these areas. I knew if I truly wanted to succeed, I needed to figure out what blind spots were holding me back!

I've just shared a lot of information. This is a good opportunity to take a moment and consider your life. Think about and answer the following questions.

In what areas of your life do you feel challenged? Why?

_____

_____

_____

_____

Who do you know that would give you honest feedback?

_____

_____

_____

_____

How will uncovering these blind spots make a difference in your life?

_____

_____

_____

_____

I hope you have taken action with these questions to work on developing a higher level of self-awareness. This will give you the ability to explore more of who you are as a person. Knowing how we learn and understanding the ***Knowns and Unknowns*** in our lives provides us the insight to move toward living our lives with intention.

CHAPTER 4

LIVING LIFE WITH INTENTION

*"Over time, even the tiniest meaningful actions add up,
each one bringing you closer to a life that is truer
to your dreams and free of regret."*

— *Jane McGonigal, SuperBetter: The Power of Living
Gamefully*

So far, we've explored the importance of developing a personal inventory checklist of what is ***"Working"*** and what is ***"Not Working,"*** opening the door to self-awareness in numerous aspects of life. You have learned how to become aware of the ***Knowns and Unknowns*** and how blind spots could be holding you back. But it takes more to achieve that ***1% More*** lifestyle and mindset. You must also decide to live your life with intention. Through the power of intention, you can set your mental energy to be focused on achieving more.

There are two types of intent: ***Good Intentions*** and ***Intentional Living.***

We all have ***Good Intentions***. For instance, you may have the good intention of starting your own business, traveling the world, or saving up money for an exotic getaway. Sadly, good intentions are usually just *fantasy, wishes, somedays,* and **hope.** We mean to do more or do better. But having a good intention is a passive act, often coupled with **"one day..."**

> *One day I will find that special someone.*
>
> *One day I will save enough money.*
>
> *One day I will travel the world.*
>
> *One day I will own my own business.*
>
> *One day...*
>
> *One day...*

What happens when "one day" never comes? You become more frustrated and less fulfilled. Remember, *"The road to hell is paved with good intentions."* Stop allowing your dreams to remain further and further out of reach. Evaluate your life, begin to plan, and take action!

Life is always on the go, go, go! We tend to live our lives on autopilot, just going through the motions. It's like getting in your car after work and suddenly finding you are home, with no real memory of the trip. Your conscious mind shut down, and your subconscious mind took over; this is how many people live their lives: asleep!

On the other hand, **Intentional Living** moves your life out of fantasy and into reality. It empowers you to take small and purposeful steps. It allows you to closely examine your choices and adjust them accordingly. It's about you exploring your "Why," your significant purpose, that feeling which compels you regardless of the sacrifice. Your "Why" is connected to your core values, and intentional living helps get you there.

Intentional living turns off autopilot and provides you with a plan to take advantage of the countless opportunities that arise when you pay attention to people and circumstances. You can achieve an unapologetic lifestyle that reflects your values, beliefs, and goals by making willful, deliberate, and consistent changes. It is not about having everything figured out, but about having a purpose behind your actions. You no longer have to rely on the idea of "one day." Focus and begin today!

Here are questions to help you to begin to live intentionally…

What are my core values and beliefs? Are they still relevant to me today?

_____

_____

_____

_____

What is my "why"? What is the big purpose that moves me to take action?

_____

_____

_____

_____

What steps can I take to start living intentionally and make my "why" come to life?

_____

_____

_____

_____

We have covered a lot so far to gain an understanding of awareness and there is a lot more to come. If you need to take a moment and catch your breath please do so, our journey has only just begun! It is time to view other aspects of awareness and continue to be awakened along our quest. The amazing individuals selected for this section will now provide you with more insight on topics of aligning your life, being you, living in wonder, understanding how to lead with purpose, and even learning a little magic!

CHAPTER 5

THE UNSPOKEN TRUTH: BE THE REAL YOU

By Teresa Porter

"Find windows of opportunities instead of making excuses."

— Teresa Porter

Do you ever wonder, *"Am I good enough? Am I deserving?"* How often do these thoughts consume you, affect your confidence, and keep you from trying something new?

These questions dominated my life as a mom, a wife, and a business owner. I tried to excel at everything, which left me feeling overwhelmed, frustrated, and not good enough or deserving of success. I discovered that when I sought out external approval, validation, and praise, it left me wondering: *Am I good enough? Am I deserving?* I asked if it, and frankly if I, were *good enough.*

Modern society insists that we seek approval, validation, and praise from the external rather than the internal. Over the years, I let the approval of others dictate my level of confidence and equated my business success as a measure of my happiness and worth.

As a working massage therapist since 1999, I have heard personal accounts that have made me laugh, cry, and render me speechless. I realized that so many, including myself, are terrified to let go of the facades or masks we wear because of modern societal expectations. Because of this, it can leave us feeling stuck, empty, lost, and on autopilot. We all have challenges and obstacles we are trying to overcome. But unfortunately, these challenges get in the way of the life we want, the one we deserve. If this is the case, *why is it so hard to attain?*

I have observed that most of my clients, especially women, have an apparent lack of self-care, specifically how they address their own needs. These unattended needs can lead to diseases, dysfunction, and chronic pain in their bodies. I recognized that the same negative patterns my clients struggled with, I saw within myself. The moment I knew things needed to change was in the summer of 2007.

The saying, *"when it rains, it pours,"* is an understatement when describing one of the most challenging times in my life. I discovered I was pregnant with our third child (unplanned but joyful), and my husband was laid off from his lucrative corporate position (our primary source of income). In the following months, we lost our house to foreclosure, a car to repossession, subsisted off my husband's 401k and credit cards and had to file for bankruptcy. Once the material objects got stripped away, I realized the possessions, the proverbial house with the white picket fence, did not define me. This time forced me to focus internally and find the strength to get through that difficult time and face the *"patterns"* by which I lived.

Despite all of the heightened emotions I felt, I needed to start listening to what my heart and gut were telling me. I realized I needed to make time for stillness. I had to be proactive about my future in thought, intention, and the language I used when speaking.

The first step in listening to my intuition was when I invested in a self-help program that cost $1,000.00. Over the 20-week course, I became conscious of my thoughts and self-talk. I surrounded myself with like-minded people. I continuously listened to audiobooks in-depth to learn more about the power of the subconscious. I started a daily gratitude practice and made daily vision goals. I knew that I had to rise above my current situation and positively carry myself, not only for me but for my daughters.

By implementing what I had learned, I started to see change, which allowed me to make positive shifts in my relationships. The stress began to dissipate. My husband and I began to talk positively and optimistically about our future.

Nearly losing everything made me realize how much of my life was lived on autopilot. There is power in becoming conscious of the way we live our lives. And although I found my mantra, my life has not been a series of accomplishments and successes. Along the way, I struggled with chronic pain, self-doubt, depression, and anxiety. At times, I became exhausted and began losing myself again. I recognized a familiar pattern emerging. When these negative recurring patterns occur, we need to take the time to look at ourselves as a whole.

Often, we don't, *so why not?*

We are scared to slow down and reflect on what's working and what isn't. That fear leads to not being in tune with what we need and desire. Autopilot becomes the path of least resistance; however, it prevents you from living optimal lives. Being stuck in the cycle of being "*busy*" does not serve us.

I used to think I did not have time to be still, meditate, or make appointments for self-care because I was too *"busy."* I knew I had to pay attention to the warning signs my body was giving before I shut down. By learning to slow down and quiet our minds, we can reflect inwardly and listen to what our bodies, hearts, and souls are saying. Once we have heard the message, we have to have the courage to act.

After seeing these life patterns within myself and my clients, I felt very inspired to design a formula that could remove the noise in our lives. This formula, my antidote, is called *"The Porter Method."* This new methodology utilizes emotional release techniques by integrating physical movement with inner peace work. The variables of my formula require you to learn how to release your subconscious blocks, align with your authentic self, and give you the tools to reset and create a life by design.

I'll be sharing two principles of this method that you can implement today. This will help you turn off autopilot, find stillness, and reconnect to your authentic self.

The first principle, called the ***Power Hour***, is an hour to rejuvenate yourself mentally, emotionally, and physically. I recommend doing your power hour first thing in the morning before checking your phone, emails, news, etc. Include the following in your Power Hour.

Power Hour- To start your day.

- *Healthy Physical Movement- At least 20 minutes a day.*

- *Meditation- Start with one to five minutes.*

- *Ten minutes to Confidence- Write down three things that you are proud of and three things that you are grateful for and why.*

The second principle practice, ***Transforming the Relationship with Self***, is meant to be practiced daily - I recommend incorporating it into your ***Power Hour***. It will help you learn to check in with your feelings and emotions and give them a voice. This practice is done by asking yourself two simple questions and journaling those responses.

- *How am I feeling?*

- *And what do I need?*

When I started this practice, I learned to slow down and fulfill my needs without feeling guilty. Sometimes those needs were as simple as allowing me to nap or treat myself to lunch. I also learned to ask my husband or kids to help with daily tasks. I know you may think you don't have an hour a day for you, but you DO!

Think about your own life and answer the following questions...

What patterns do you see in your own life?

_____

_____

_____

_____

_____

_____

What is your intuition telling you that you are not listening to?

_____

_____

_____

_____

_____

_____

How are you feeling? And what do you need?

_____

_____

_____

_____

_____

_____

As a special gift, I am offering a download to my **Ten Minutes To Confidence** prompts and my **Five To Thrive** self-care outline at ***www. sirrineyoga.com/unpluggedresources***

ABOUT THE AUTHOR

Teresa Porter was born and raised in Gilbert, Arizona. She is a dedicated wife, mother of three, and a business owner, turning her dreams into reality.

Teresa has worked in the health and fitness industry for over 22 years as a massage therapist, yoga instructor, and emotional release practitioner. Working as a massage therapist since 1999, she has seen firsthand how negative trapped emotions and lack of self-care contribute to physical issues.

Teresa's love and dedication to the craft make her a maven in the industry. Her expertise will take you on a journey of self-awareness by working through negative patterns and transforming them into positive ones.

Known as The Porter Method, Teresa's new methodology utilizes emotional release techniques including integrating physical movement, and inner peace work that helps release subconscious blocks to help reset and create a life by design.

To learn more, go to www.sirrineyoga.come/unpluggedresources

AUTHOR CONTACT INFORMATION

Teresa Porter, *Owner of Sirrine Yoga & Emotional Release Practitioner*

Website: www.sirrineyoga.com

Email: teresa@sirrinestudio.com

Social: @sirrineyoga (Facebook, Instagram, Pinterest, Twitter, YouTube)

https://www.linkedin.com/in/teresa-porter-yoga-instructor-743b7858

Business phone number: 480-510-1203

CHAPTER 6

SELF-ALIGNMENT COACHING

By Agne Paceviciute

"There is no good or bad, right or wrong, nice or nasty.
There is only who we really are, and who we think we are.
Don't listen to the lies of the mind, listen to the truth
in the heart. Only love is real."

— *Julia Hardy*

Are you one of the people who strongly desire to do something great in this world yet struggle to discover your purpose? Have you had some great experiences and realize you are still scratching the surface of what's possible for you? Do you feel like something is blocking you from living your true potential, and are you ready to change that?

I know how that feels. I've been stuck for years searching for my true self. I was ashamed that I didn't know who I am; I felt unworthy, not enough, a complete failure. At some point, I realized I didn't want to live that way, so I started my journey back to self. I had been searching for answers outside of myself—new business, new car, new house—these prizes were supposed to make me happy. Then I discovered that I had a crowd of limiting beliefs blocking my way to achieve all my desires. I went looking for answers to reprogram my mind, to reach the subconscious. I tried so many techniques and methods with no significant results. Until one day, everything clicked. I experienced that deep unconditional love and happiness coming from within. I knew then that my life would never be the same again, and I felt so passionate to share this message with every person in the world.

You are a wonderful being with enormous potential; everything is possible for you to achieve. Do you believe it? Tapping into your highest version requires reorganizing your Human Operating System, transforming any limiting beliefs, and mastering your inner power. You may ask, *"How can I do that?"* I am here to tell you how.

Imagine how our brain works very similarly to a computer. From childhood, the people around us program us to follow certain behaviors and beliefs. Until we are six or seven years of age, our brains operate in a hypnotic state, absorbing all the information without filtering out anything. We learn to become compliant in family, community, society, culture, religion, and other social structures. We fit ourselves into an often-limiting environment. We believe in our limitations, and we learn to follow the rules without questioning them.

What if those limitations are not real? What if you are capable of expressing so much more? What if your beliefs and thinking patterns limit your life experience, and it's possible to create a reality of your dreams?

Emotions are chemical reactions triggered by the electric impulses firing neurons in a thought process, creating the thinking and feeling loop. When this process becomes habitual, it is called a belief. Because the belief has a mental and physical element, we can say it is energetically stored somewhere inside your body.

We generally describe the mind as two parts: conscious and sub-conscious. We are only aware of 5-15% of the information registered by our brain. Up to 95% of our brain function is dedicated to our subconscious programs and beliefs. In the computer analogy, the screen represents the conscious mind you can see, and you have limited control of the programs. The subconscious is a hard drive where all the programs are stored, and they completely control what appears on the screen. Subconscious programs are like filters to our life experiences.

For example, if you believe that money is hard to come by, you will have a hard time with finances, and money will be scarce. No matter how hard you try, the belief that you are not good enough will not allow you to have a better job position. Similarly, believing that you are not lovable will make harmonious relationships nearly impossible. In no way is this your fault; your life experience registers a subconscious program that automatically plays out.

There are many limiting programs, from early childhood and later in life through traumatic experiences. Because we are conscious of about 5% of information received, that leaves 95% out of our awareness. The stories you decided to believe early on, and the meaning you gave (and continue to give) to your experiences, are based on your programming. Therefore, it all plays out: Your brain filters out great opportunities to make money easily; your potential employer senses your doubt about your abilities, so you don't get your dream job; your program "I'm not lovable" guides you to partners who have no intention to love you.

So, how to solve this problem? How to reprogram our minds and change our life into the line of brilliant experiences? Let me present a tool that gave me and my clients the fastest and most significant results. Forget about listening to affirmations year after year; you can transform your limiting beliefs in minutes.

Quantum Healing is an energy healing practice based on the NLP structure. Neuro-Linguistic Programming, as you may know, studies subjective human experiences based on the mind and body connection. Using NLP tools, Quantum Healing takes it several steps forward in the energy realm. The transformation happens instantly and typically resolves the issue for good, so you don't need to keep managing it. Quantum Healing is not a management technique—it is a resolution strategy.

Opening up the communication process between your mind, body, and spirit engages your healing abilities, intuition, self-love, and more of your inner resources, which helps you rearrange the neural pathways in the brain, removing the blockages. It provides you with a past, present, and future structure that allows you to resolve trauma. The Quantum Healing Self-Alignment program activates your energy centers. Connecting to your higher self, accelerates the manifestation of your desires.

Quantum Healing has a broad range of tools helping to transform multiple issues. From healing the inner child or resolving relationship issues to downloading information from the future or channeling from alternative dimensions. The possibilities in the Quantum Field are expansive.

Imagine if you could dissolve the limiting beliefs holding you back for years; imagine breaking free from any imposed limitations. How would your life be different if you were connected to your intuition and fully aligned with your higher self? How would you feel experiencing unconditional love and happiness for life? There is no better experience than going from depression and worthlessness to spiritual awakening and activating your superpowers. Life is so much more meaningful and fulfilling on the other side of struggle and fear. Please don't take my word for it! Choose to explore your inner world and expansive possibilities in the Quantum Field.

My friend, I welcome you to a journey that will transform your life and increase your positive impact in the world. When you approach it with open-mindedness, curiosity, and non-judgment, you will discover wonders you never knew existed within you. When you are in alignment, you will lovingly see the powerful being you are and have always been—pure love and light.

Begin to get your life in alignment, and answer the following questions...

What events trigger emotions that cause you to immediately respond?

_____

_____

_____

_____

What beliefs are you holding onto that no longer serve you?

_____

_____

_____

_____

How would you feel experiencing unconditional love and happiness for life?

_____

_____

_____

_____

About The Author

Agne Paceviciute, a Sweden-based, Lithuania-born Self-Alignment Coach and Quantum Healing Facilitator, started her self-discovery journey by realizing that she lived her life by other people's standards and failed to express her authentic self.

Over the years of self-search, she completed an M.Sc. (Master of Science) in Biophysics in 2009. Expanding her knowledge in brain science and exploring spirituality helped her discover life's purpose as she was desperately searching for ways to fix herself, release false programming, and feel more in touch with herself. By following numerous personal development gurus and success teachers, learning about behavior science and Quantum Physics, experimenting with many techniques, she hoped to find a sustainable process to hack the subconscious mind. Her dream came true.

One day a line of beautiful synchronicities took her to the most profound spiritual awakening experience. Soon after, she came across a transformational method to help others awaken and experience indescribable alignment in mind, body, and spirit. It felt like the abundance flew into her life through different pathways that instantly shattered multiple blocks. After those profound shifts, she immediately began learning the Quantum Healing Process with various tools to help transform many issues.

In 2020, Agne became one of three certified practitioners worldwide. She has helped many people release mental blocks, heal past traumas, and discover the enormous power they have within. Agne continues to learn and leads by example, inspiring people to recognize their unlimited potential.

AUTHOR CONTACT INFORMATION

Agne Paceviciute, *Self-Alignment Coach and Quantum Healing Facilitator*
Website: www.self-alignment-coaching.com
Email: agne@self-alignment-coaching.com
Social: www.facebook.com/Self-Alignment-Coaching-102442071785473

STOP CHASING JOY BEGIN LIVING IN WONDER!

By Dr. Karthik Ramanan

"Have the courage to follow your heart and intuition.
They somehow know what you truly want to become.
Everything else is secondary."

— *Steve Jobs*

You walk up to the window of your 30th floor skyrise apartment. As you gaze into the sunset on the horizon, the feeling of gratitude overcomes you. You are blessed with a career that has allowed you to pay off all your student loan debt. You give more to charity each year than you ever thought possible. You are recognized and rewarded as a high achiever in your field.

I found myself living that very life at the age of 27. On the surface, I had it all.

Beneath the surface, though, lay a serious problem. I hated the man in the mirror.

My overweight body made me cower in shame. My eyes told the story of utter loneliness. My life severely lacked meaningful purpose.

On the outside, I was a high-performing Ivy League graduate working on Wall Street in New York. I had it all together.

But on the inside, nobody knew just how my self-critical mind savaged my confidence, my presence, and my joy.

After years of failed diets and extreme exercise programs, a sinking feeling crept over me.

"Is this all there is for me? Has my time run out?"

I hit rock bottom.

However, rock bottom is a beautiful place to be. Rock bottom is the point at which we are willing to try anything. Rock bottom is the moment at which we will take massive action. Rock bottom is the chance to discover who we truly are.

My rock bottom aligned beautifully with a visit with my sister. Since I had last seen her, she had lost 30 pounds, cleared up her skin, and reinvigorated her life. Whatever she had done, I had to do the same! She told me about this raw food plant-based diet she had adopted. She ate only uncooked, fresh fruits, vegetables, nuts and seeds. I thought abiding by such a diet was crazy, but I committed to it anyway. After all, what did I have to lose?

One hundred pounds later, I had inspired countless people to take life into their own hands and uncover their inner power. I decided that my next few years resided not on Wall Street but in medical school, studying to become a naturopathic physician.

When I flew out to Arizona for the next chapter of my life, I realized that nobody knew me. This was my chance to define who Dr. K of the future would be. How does he think? How does he eat? How does he move? How does he treat others? What are his habits, routines, mindsets, and beliefs? I defined this man, and I lived into that vision every day. I pushed myself outside my comfort zone repeatedly. I released who I thought I should be and embraced who I truly am. I stopped living in circumstance, and I started living in the wonder of the man I could be.

In the process, the man who was too ashamed of himself to leave his apartment over the weekends became the man with the confidence and growth mentality to become magnetic to the perfect woman for him. Those countless years of loneliness and self-criticism were worth it. They were necessary for me to change, to become the man with whom my future wife would fall in love.

We spend too much time focusing on things we cannot control, trying to become the person we think we are supposed to be. We pretend everything is ok by out-working and out-achieving everyone else, just to hide from ourselves. We wear the badge of overachiever and perfectionist to give ourselves no chance to sit in silence with the thoughts in our minds.

That is no way to live.

Let today be the day you declare to stop chasing joy. Make your joy. Let today be the day you stop resigning to circumstance. Live in wonder. Stop making yourself feel like a failure. Instead, live with purpose.

The shy guy who put on a face to be a high achiever for the world should never have become the Dr. K that I am today.

If you mastered your emotional health, what could you do?

Many of us walk around telling ourselves we are fine.

"How are you doing today?"

"Fine."

Are you? To yourself, when nobody's watching, are you truly fine? I know you have goals and aspirations, great things you want to do in this world. Maybe you have convinced yourself that you need to work on yourself first. Maybe you have convinced yourself that your time will come. Maybe you have convinced yourself that you are happy enough right now.

Maybe in the middle of chronically binging Netflix, numbing your racing mind with food and alcohol, and withdrawing yourself from meaningful human conversation, you quietly start to wonder, "Is this all there is? Am I just broken?"

You are worth more than that! You were not born into this world to go through all you have endured just to sit and hope things will get better. Seize it! Your time is now! Do you want joy in your life? You can have it! Do you want that fit body? Go create it! Do you want to finally live that dream you have had all your life, the one you put on the backburner to "do the right thing"? Go live it!

The bad news is that only you have the power to get out of your own way. Nobody can do it for you. The good news is, you don't have to wait for a special time or anyone. Decide in this moment that enough is enough. Take one small step toward the person you were born to be. Don't wait for life to happen to you. Make your life happen for you.

Imagine you're a block of ice at zero degrees Fahrenheit: frozen in place and stuck. You want nothing more than to reach 32 degrees and beyond so you can become water: powerful, flowing, and free.

You dive into the world of personal development. You read the books, listen to the podcasts, and go to the seminars. Maybe you generate the courage to go to therapy or see a doctor. You get warmer and warmer. 10 degrees. 15 degrees. 20 degrees. But somewhere around 25 degrees, you feel stuck, exhausted, and burned out. You do your affirmations, exercise, and eat right. Yet you feel blind to your progress despite the years of effort you've put in. It feels like you're still at 0 degrees.

But is it that one degree from 31 to 32 that makes the state change from ice to water? NO! It is the latent potential energy that accumulates as you add heat to the ice cube that eventually breaks through at 32 degrees. That work you have put in has greatly benefited you. But the work that it took you to go from zero to 25 is not the same work that it takes to go from 25 to 32. It takes a new method. It takes a new mentality. It takes a mentor.

I'm Dr. K, your emotional health mentor. Stop chasing joy. Begin living in wonder. I believe in your greatness!

Master your emotional health with my online workshops, my intensive one-to-one mentoring program, or my emotional health benefit program for employers at https://drkarthikramanan.com

Begin to live your life in wonder and be in action, answer the following questions…

How do you currently view yourself in the mirror? What do you like? What don't you like?

_____

_____

_____

_____

_____

_____

What massive action can you take, right now, that can make a difference in your life?

_____

_____

_____

_____

_____

How can you begin to live in wonder and create your own joy?

_____

_____

_____

_____

_____

About The Author

Dr. Karthik Ramanan, NMD ("Dr. K") is a licensed Naturopathic Physician and your Emotional Health Mentor.

Dr. K completed his undergraduate studies at Cornell University with dual bachelor's degrees in Biological Sciences and Applied Economics and Management.

He went on to work eight years on Wall Street, a period of time that spanned the recession of 2008 and the years after. After experiencing a life-changing 100-pound weight loss journey, he left his career and attended Southwest College of Naturopathic Medicine in Tempe, Arizona to become a naturopathic physician.

Today, Dr. K is committed to helping other high-achieving entrepreneurs and professionals end burnout so that they can stop chasing joy and begin living in wonder.

AUTHOR CONTACT INFORMATION

Dr. Karthik Ramanan, NMD ("Dr. K") *is a licensed Naturopathic Physician and your Emotional Health Mentor.*
Website: drkarthikramanan.com
Email: karthik@vicarium.com
Social: @drkarthikramanan (Linkedin, YouTube)
Instagram: instagram.com/dr.karthikramanan
Clubhouse: @drknmd

CHAPTER 8

MINDSET WILL LEAD YOU TO YOUR PURPOSE

By Allison Noelle Megherian

"I hope there are days where you fall in love with being alive. I hope part of your heart lives there forever."

— Unknown

What is happening in your mind is a direct reflection of what is happening around you. You can sit and decide that you have no control of what's going on in your life or you can TAKE control. Your mind, and your energy are so incredibly powerful.

They are the ONLY things you CAN control.

So why is it that we don't allow ourselves to take this control and live the life of our dreams? It is the question that led me to becoming a Life/Mindset coach. We live in a society built around limiting beliefs, expectations, and negative perceptions. The environment we surround ourselves with highly influences our decisions rather than allowing our minds, intuition, passion, and purpose to guide our life decision making.

We worry so much about what is GOING to happen and are less focused on how far we have come and what we have now.

My entire life I was always asking myself these questions,

- *Will I achieve success?*
- *Will I have enough money?*
- *Will I meet the one?*
- *Will I make my family proud?*
- *Will others approve of my decisions?*
- *Will I ever be enough?*

Do you find that you have this mindset?

A mindset of how you are viewed by others is how you control your life?

Many will not even admit that they do. We are raised in a world of social media that validation by likes, comments, and wealth are how we measure if we are living a good life.

Inner Peace: The Secret To Purpose

The day I found true inner peace was an epiphany. I was always a happy person, a bubbly kid growing up, had friends and a FANTASTIC family. But as I grew up, I realized I wasn't happy internally. I didn't understand how to make myself happy. I am a musician and truly a performer. I performed my whole life to make sure everyone around me approved of my decisions. I did give a lot of push back and did chase my dreams but never to the fullest extent. Being a dreamer as a child is cute to many adults but as you get older dreams aren't as big and the support fades.

The adult life of being "realistic" about my dreams quickly swept in and it took me in multiple directions. I had to "play it safe" which is something that has been taught through many generations. Our parents/society never want us to "fail" and want us to be able to support ourselves and live a full life. I questioned this at a young age, to "play it safe" didn't mean that I would be happy. My dreams weren't safe, and I knew that to make my dreams a reality, I'd have to work extra hard.

I had lots of ups and downs throughout my career. I started out wanting to be a full-time singer, and then became a full-time music teacher. This was not at all what I had in mind. I knew and understood that it was a SAFE decision. At the time I didn't understand this part of my journey. When I was teaching and making music in my spare time, I was so unhappy. My mind-body connection was off, I was so worried about what everyone was thinking, and I really hit the point that I didn't even like myself. So, the happy girl who had it all going for her was MISERABLE. Many didn't notice, I hid it well and distracted myself by working 24/7, partying with friends and ignoring everything my intuition was telling me.

Intuition

What the heck is that?! It's your gut! Your true inner feeling and knowing. My gut was telling me things and my mind was blocked with every limiting belief. I was never going to be good enough, I was never going to have enough money for anything, I was never going to find love, I was never going to live the life of my dreams. WRONG- The pity party inside my head was a daily routine that I knew needed to stop. That awareness was the driving force for me to make the change.

I knew it would be work but I needed to declutter my mind. I started with decluttering what I was putting in my body, cleaned up my diet, stopped partying as often. The shift was happening! I was losing weight, looking, and feeling better. I started realizing how badly

I was treating myself and couldn't calm my mind. I started reading more books about life, the universe and found Kundalini Meditation. I could finally breathe. The clearing was happening, and I was fully present in my body. My "aha moment" of realizing this is inner peace, this is gratitude for being alive. Now to find out, why am I here?

Motivating the Mindset: Shifting and rewiring your journey

When I made the decision to take my power back and shift my mindset, it was unreal how quickly everything in my life started to change. I started becoming aware of how and why I was on my journey. As a teacher, I started incorporating mindfulness into my daily routine with my students. I knew my life was becoming better and felt it was important to teach it to them. I even published a motivational book for kids through this process. I became aware that at the end of the day, we are all equal. Only I can control my thoughts and the only thing blocking me from doing that was myself. I changed my perception on all things in my life. I continued to write and record music with more meaning. I started doing this for ME and no one else.

Life was happening FOR me! I never failed, I LEARNED. I realized that finding happiness and purpose had to come from within. Every part of my journey that came from a good intention, allowed me to grow, and evolve into the person I was always meant to be. I rewire my brain everyday with being in nature daily, practicing kundalini meditation, journaling, reflecting, setting healthy boundaries, having solo dance parties, and enjoying wine with my family and friends to celebrate life.

Another epiphany, I must share this with the world! I want to teach/ help others find inner peace, real happiness that has nothing to do with society except for their purpose on this earth. I want people to know that you can wake up happy even if you are not married, you don't have children and you are not yet at your dream job. All of your dreams CAN be a reality. I have accomplished more in my life than I ever thought possible. My life is balanced, my mindset is clear, and it led me to my purpose. I continue to do the work on myself and make myself a priority every day. I officially have a coaching business and am living my purpose. ANYTHING is possible, take back your power, level up your life and motivate your mindset.

Let's have your mindset lead you to your purpose; answer the following questions...

How is your mind holding you back?

_____

_____

_____

_____

_____

What is your intuition telling you that you're not listening too?

_____

_____

_____

_____

_____

What lights you up? What dream do you want to make into a reality?

_____

_____

_____

_____

_____

ABOUT THE AUTHOR

Allison Noelle Megherian is a Mindset Mentor and Motivational Speaker for "Motivating the Mindset".

Allison is also an author of the book " A Motivational Reset for the Mindset" for young adults and a Music Teacher in NYC. She is from Long Island, New York where she received her bachelor's degree in Vocal performance at Adelphi University.

In addition, Allison is a singer, songwriter and recording artist. She received her Master's Degrees from Hofstra University in Music Education and another Master's Degree in Educational Leadership from The College of Saint Rose. Through mindset tools and breathwork, Allison helps you rewire your brain, connect your mind and body to gain clarity and control of your life!

AUTHOR CONTACT INFORMATION

Allison Noelle Megherian, *Mindset Mentor and Motivational Speaker*
Website: AllisonNoelleMotivation.com
Email: MotivatingTheMindset@gmail.com
Social: Allison.Noelle_ (Instagram)

CHAPTER 9

HOW I LEARNED PURE F**KIN' MAGIC™

By Nadine Sabulsky

"Any sufficiently advanced technology is indistinguishable from magic."

— Arthur C. Clarke

The first schism with my family's faith happened in fourth grade, when my Christian-school teacher and principal prayed over me for the 'sin' of wearing pink nail polish. I thought, "Does God really care that much if I color my nails???"

At age ten, I discovered my first universal principle – there is no such thing as only one 'right way.' I discovered this while reading a science-fiction story. It thrilled me, because even at a young age I was mentally rebelling against the expectations that "good girls" grow up, get married, and have kids. I never wanted to get married, I wanted to grow up, become a career woman, and travel the world!

I got hooked on sci-fi and that, in turn, led me into many of my life-long passions, human potential, metaphysics, sociology, science and technology. I also loved reading epic fantasy and became fascinated with the idea that perhaps magic is real, and we're just trained from a young age to ignore and suppress it.

From these two early loves, my journey has been to explore the intersection of magic and technology. Here's an interesting fact that not many people know – the word 'technology' doesn't just mean computers, machines, cars, etc., the actual dictionary definition of technology is 'applied knowledge'. Clarke's third law (quoted above) inspired me to believe that magic and technology may truly be interchangeable terms.

By age thirteen, I decided to rebel against the church completely, and I became a Wiccan. I wasn't attracted to nor worshiping any Gods/Goddesses or deities, but I loved learning about and practicing magic.

The few spells I did worked, yet, by age fifteen, I realized that all those rituals were simply training wheels for our minds to accept the idea that we can influence our reality. I began to fully focus on honing just two things: my will and my word.

Over the course of the next ten years, I studied and traveled, finally finding my home at Phoenix Arizona in mid- 2000.

In 2007, right before my life fell apart, I watched 'The Secret', and I suddenly recognized that I had not been applying my magic to very much at all – there were many more possibilities and ways to use it!

Another universal truth revealed: the only limiter we have is our imagination, or lack thereof.

I immediately began applying this "Law of Attraction stuff" to more things in my life. One of the very first was changing my traffic setting since I used to commute five hours to work in Las Vegas over the weekend. Going that thirty-mile stretch of two-lane over the Hoover Dam was invariably frustrating! Yet, suddenly, like magic, the roads cleared, and traffic flowed smoothly and quickly wherever and whenever I drove!

I applied manifestation in more and more ways, and I was (seemingly) really getting the hang of it, when suddenly my life got smashed to bits.

First, a heartbreaking split with the awesomest person I'd ever dated.

Then, the crash of 2008 nearly wiped me out financially. I had been making a comfortable income of around $4,000/month from my two businesses, and in one month it went to $1,500, and the next month I was barely scraping $1,000.

I lost my driver's license because I couldn't afford the license plate renewal, on a car that would be repossessed two months after the expiration date.

I struggled to stay in my home, but that too was lost to foreclosure a few months later. If not for the grace of a dear friend, I would have been homeless at that point.

Throughout this trying time, I was still doing all I could to master manifestation. I knew there was something to it because I had successfully manifested many things in my life so far. Yet now it seemed I was having just as much skill de-manifesting things from my life!

"What," I wondered, "is the difference between the things I've manifested quite easily, and the things I've had difficulty with or been unable to manifest, or have even de-manifested?"

I had finally asked the right question! During deep meditation on that question, while reviewing all the manifestations and "de-manifestations" (I know now that both are technically manifestations), I began to see the commonalities.

These commonalities eventually became my first book about conscious manifestation, 'Living the Naked Life: 10 Ways to Expose Your Unlimited Creation Abilities.' But what I didn't know at the time was that one core component tied everything together: emotions.

When I began my 'dream job' and first started coaching people about manifestation, I focused mostly on helping people change their thoughts and their words. In fact, most gurus today still preach positive thinking as "the one right way." Yet, changing all our thoughts is much more difficult than you might 'think!'

"Experts estimate that the mind thinks between 60,000 – 80,000 thoughts a day. That's an average of 2500 – 3,300 thoughts per hour. That's incredible. Other experts estimate a smaller number, of 50,000 thoughts per day, which means about 2100 thoughts per hour." – Success Consciousness

Wait… 50,000 thoughts – PER DAY???

Nobody has time to spend policing and changing that many thoughts!

As I coached people, I saw much faster results when I showed them how to master their emotions first. In fact, whenever I consciously manifested things, I know with certainty that it was because I was in emotional alignment with my goals.

Now, through the power of "practicing what I preach," I've manifested my dream lifestyle, met my perfect partner, moved into my mini-mansion, and worked with amazing people all over the world to facilitate their own dream life makeover!

After teaching these principles since 2010, I can easily summarize **Pure Fuckin' Magic™** with one simple sentence…

You get more of whatever you focus on, and your foci are your beliefs, thoughts, feelings/emotions, words, and actions.

Most teachers, trainers and therapists rely on teaching you new beliefs, and focus on helping you change your thoughts and modify your actions. No one teaches us how to consciously control and change our own emotions! Yet, emotions are much easier to train, and by doing so we provide a support framework that makes changing all our beliefs, thoughts, words, and actions sooooo much easier!

In fact, when we master our emotions, life does indeed become quite magical!

The thing is, like me in 2009, all of us are addicted to stress of one type or another. I say addicted because each emotion produces a bio-chemical state in the body, and our bodies become habituated to that state!

Then what happens is our subconscious gets involved. See, our sub-conscious is a very helpful tool – but it's a DUMB tool! Subcon-scious doesn't know any better, it just strives to give the body what it craves.

The key is to reprogram our biochemistry AND our subconscious mind, and doing so takes only one month, through training alone. No drugs, no supplements, just brain retraining.

Learn to create your own magic, and answer the following questions...

How would you like to influence your reality?

_____

_____

_____

_____

With no limitations on your imagination, what would you create if nothing was stopping you?

_____

_____

_____

_____

What amazing wonder would you manifest in your life?

_____

_____

_____

_____

To learn more about this and other mental health topics, get my latest book, '*Uncovering 13 Common Myths of Traditional Therapy,*' FREE for a limited time on my website.

About The Author

Nadine's genius lies in synergistically combining metaphysics, neuroscience, psychology, sociology, and cultural history, and extracting the key underlying principles of self-mastery. She deftly guides her clientele to; eliminate their unwanted stressors, streamline their creativity, and systematically focus on exactly what they want, while filling in any missing skill sets to their repertoire, and from there they are easily able to cultivate their authentic magic and escape the mundane repression of the mainstream, cookie-cutter world, so they can realize their full potential and truly be free to live out their wildest dreams in reality!

Rising from her humble beginnings in a conservative religious household, Nadine has been a lifelong and adventurous entrepreneur with 9 businesses in multiple industries to date, developed her own coaching modality, created an innovative curative approach to mental health, has published 8 transformative books, and her feedback from clients is unsurpassed. In 2021 she was reviewed and ranked as the #1 A+ rated life coach in Scottsdale Arizona by Expertise.com. She has been featured on ABC, FOX, and numerous podcasts and magazines. Nadine's channels have 1M+ views, and she's been featured as a #1 best seller on Amazon.

What sets Nadine apart from other gurus and experts is not only the breadth and depth of her gathered wisdom, but also her ability to communicate even the most abstract concepts in simple, everyday language and provide practical easy applications of her esoteric knowledge, for the joyous enhancement of every part of life. She guides her clients step-by-step to curate their mind, body and spirit, and create a "life-style by design."

Fascinated by human potential, magic and science, Nadine's life journey has played at the nexus of mysticism and technology. "Reality is eminently mutable", she explains. "We are creating and co-creating the reality we inhabit regularly. The question is, do you want to continue to do that randomly and unconsciously, or do you want to learn how to take control, and consciously create the things that you truly desire to experience?"

Nadine loves working with eccentric and creative individuals who are committed to maximizing their full potential and passionate about transforming the world into a better place for all of us. Her clients are a mix of high performing executives and successful entrepreneurs who, like her previous self, feel they haven't reached their true potential, and creatives and artists who have unresolved traumas, often suffer from addictions, and carry the burden of fame. She helps them connect, heal themselves, and reach for the stars with a rejuvenated outlook on life.

Nadine's experimental approach to her own life has produced energetic health and vibrancy, abiding unconditional love, an absolutely amazing relationship with her perfect partner, many and varied lifelong friendships, 'miracles' being a normalized occurrence, an abundance of creativity and motivation, a beautiful home environment, unlimited success in business, and plenty of time to enjoy it all. She is devoted to helping others embody and activate their own inner God/Dess so they can be awesome and create the dream love, happiness, and lifestyle, they truly desire!

AUTHOR CONTACT INFORMATION

Nadine Sabulsky, *The Naked Life Coach*
Website: TheNakedLifeCoach.com
Email: nadine@thenakedlifecoach.com
Social: @NadineSabulsky (Facebook)

PILLAR TWO

GROWTH

CHAPTER 10

THE FIVE AREAS OF GROWTH

"Without continual growth and progress, such words as improvement, achievement, and success have no meaning."

— *Benjamin Franklin*

*I*f you are here, that tells me you have begun the work to gain a higher sense of awareness. As shared earlier, awareness is the first stage of your journey, where you start looking inward at who you are and figure out where you want to go. Our coaches have shared their tools and resources for becoming self-aware, and if you have taken them to heart, you are ready to continue to the next stage, **Growth**.

Learning to grow can be scary. It requires you to have courage, to create change, and to push yourself out of your comfort zone and into new uncharted waters. It may even take you to your breaking point, breaking you free of the past, the identities you have held on to, and the false beliefs you created. The beautiful part of growth is that it's a lifelong process with unlimited possibilities.

There are five areas of personal growth: *Mental, Social, Spiritual, Emotional, and Physical.*

Mental Growth - is all about expanding your mind, whether through taking classes, listening to podcasts, reading books, attending seminars, visiting a museum, traveling, or trying new experiences. Growing your mind creates opportunities for stronger relationships, broader knowledge, and advancement in your career.

Social Growth - is all about becoming a more effective communicator, forging new relationships, and improving your listening skills. Learning more about other people's communication styles is an advantageous way to build rapport and get to connect with someone. So get out and connect with someone new today, join a networking group, or watch a video that offers advice on how to communicate more effectively.

Spiritual Growth - is about connecting to your inner being and consciousness, to rise above ordinary, everyday life. It can awaken you to some truths about who you really are. It peels away some of the beliefs, thoughts, ideas, and unreal concepts that may be holding you back. Spiritual growth can help you build a more harmonious life, one of peace and free of stress, anxiety, and fear. Great ways to improve this area are to meditate fifteen minutes a day, think positively, and express gratitude for the good things in your life.

Emotional Growth - Understanding and managing your emotions is essential to helping you reach resolutions to problems and cope with unexpected and sometimes unpleasant events that come your way. Emotional growth or "emotional maturity" is something that you develop over time by taking responsibility for your feelings about yourself, others, and the world around you. If you want to live a happy and fulfilled life, you need to cultivate healthy and satisfying relationships. The way you manage setbacks, failures, and misfortunes is based upon your emotional perceptions and your responses to them. If you manage your emotions with a level head, the outcome will be a lot different than if you lose control. Strength comes from managing your emotions, taking responsibility, and acting within integrity.

Physical Growth - If you are not physically well, your mind and body cannot function at their highest levels. Physical activity is necessary to supply vital chemicals to the brain and build a more robust and healthier mind. Exercise, eating well, and sleeping 7-9 hours each night are essential parts of treating mental health problems and assist in relieving symptoms of anxiety and depression. Building the foundation of a healthy lifestyle begins with building better habits. So, let's tie up our shoelaces, put on our favorite gym shirts, grab our water bottles and head out the door for some fresh air and exercise!

If you need assistance in organizing your life to take on these five important areas of personal growth, try separating them into themed days and be intentional with each one.

Here is an example:

MONDAY	TUESDAY	WEDNESDAY	THURSDAY	FRIDAY	SATURDAY	SUNDAY
MENTAL GROWTH	SOCIAL GROWTH	PHYSICAL GROWTH	EMOTIONAL GROWTH	REFLECTION	FREE DAY	SPIRITUAL GROWTH

Each theme will keep you focused and motivated with excitement to see what opportunities await. Jumping around and dabbling in each one will get you nowhere, but being committed, consistent, and having a plan will help you achieve that *1% More!*

To enhance your journey in to growing here are a few ideas you can begin today!

- *Keep a journal*
- *Create a vision board*
- *Meditate*
- *Hire a personal trainer*
- *Find an accountability partner*
- *Hire a coach*
- *Attend a networking group*
- *Read books about personal development*
- *Attend a class, seminar, or workshop*

Let's not let your growth stop here, answer the following questions...

What ways can you grow and develop your mind? (Mental)

_____

_____

_____

_____

What networking groups or organizations can you join? (Social)

_____

_____

_____

_____

What are ways you can enhance your spiritual growth in just 15 minutes a day? (Spiritual)

_____

_____

_____

_____

What ways can enhance your emotional growth and build increased resilience when your emotions get the best of you? (Emotional)

_____

_____

_____

_____

What does wellness mean to you? What can you do today that can make an impact on your health and physical growth? (Physical)

_____

_____

_____

_____

CHAPTER 11

BE COMFORTABLE WITH BEING UNCOMFORTABLE

*"If we're growing, we're always going
to be out of our comfort zone."*

— John Maxwell

How many times have you been stuck in an uncomfortable situation? For myself, more often than I can count on two hands.

It starts with an overwhelming feeling of **_"get me out of here!"_** You begin to feel hot all over. Your palms begin to sweat. Your words don't make sense and you want to crawl under a rock. Ugh! What a horrible feeling! Right?

Your comfort zone is the situation where you feel at ease, in control, and comfortable. Once that zone gets broken, you have two choices, resist, or rise to the occasion.

I remember having an incredibly awkward conversation with my former father-in-law, about his daughter being pregnant. Talk about being out of your comfort zone! I was eighteen years old at the time. I went over to their house after my girlfriend (now former wife) broke the news. It was awkward and stressful, and I was full of anxiety. My mind was racing with different thoughts about how the situation would go, and my emotions were all over the place.

My father-in-law sat me down in his den, his private space where he enjoyed watching golf and viewing nature out his windows. I sat on the edge of a firm green chair, trying to stay composed but inside dying of fear. I wanted to run, but I knew I had to address the situation. But he was calm; he provided me words of wisdom and left me with a choice to make in my life.

At eighteen, I knew nothing about becoming a parent. I barely knew who I was. How would I raise and guide a family? I was scared. I was outside of my comfort zone in more ways than one.

I did marry his daughter, and we had our beautiful girl and raised two fantastic sons after that. Being young, we had many ups and downs and unfortunately, our marriage ultimately did not work. But I learned a lot and am very grateful for the experience. Bringing my three children into the world and watching them grow has been worth it all.

As you can see, stepping out of your comfort zone is not easy, and at times you are faced with a situation where you need to take responsibility, whether you like it or not.

The following image shows how three types of zones relate to each other.

The first circle is your *comfort zone*, where you are at ease, maybe not doing your best, but doing okay enough to be content with where you are. Unfortunately, over time, you will likely find that staying in your comfort zone is unfulfilling. Complacence may be comfortable, but it also makes you lazy. When you are not moving outside your comfort zone, there is no opportunity for growth.

You may even be in this place right now!

I wish I had a dollar for every time someone said to me *"Oh, you can't do that!"* or *"Who do you think you are?"* or *"You are going to fail!"* I'd be rich! It's no wonder that most people find it easier to stay put and not make any effort. Stepping into that unknown is hard, and it takes a lot of confidence to move forward when everyone around you doubts you. But eventually, if you don't take action to step out of your comfort zone, a situation or person will come along that gives you an ultimatum. Like it or not, you'll be forced to make a decision.

When you make an intentional choice to examine your blind spots and unknowns, you have the opportunity to grow and to learn how to deal with problems and challenges differently. Indeed, opportunity is what shuttles you toward *Growth* and the *Stretch Zone*. This shaded area is where you begin to discover what you are made of. Here you lay the groundwork for facing problem areas, learn about new skill sets, and begin to extend yourself into the *Stretch Zone*.

The *Stretch Zone* is where you will test what you have learned, grow your abilities, and gain self-confidence. You may feel uneasy at first or experience a bit of internal resistance, but that is all part of the process. Someone once said to me that if trying something new doesn't frighten you and excite you simultaneously, there is no point in doing it. So, challenge yourself!

Being in the *Stretch Zone* is about pushing yourself and testing your abilities to grow and improve. Mistakes and failing will happen and that's okay. Learn and discover something new about yourself, dive deeper into your opportunities of growth, and be open to the new possibilities.

I like to keep myself in the Stretch Zone, but at times I do feel overwhelmed and maybe a little bit panicky. I feel like I may have gone outside of my limits, and maybe walking a fine line between success and failure. This is an area of *Risk*. I have been here many times, starting a business, writing a book, having a family, changing careers. I begin to worry and remember other people's doubts about me. Concern that I have made a wrong decision makes me tense, frustrated, and even angry. I tell myself not to panic! Perhaps you know from your own experiences that that is easier said than done, right?

You know you've crossed from *Risk* into the *Panic Zone* when you can no longer keep your thoughts and emotions in line. You are so overwhelmed with fear that your ability to learn and plan gets stifled. You are driven mostly by emotion and a sense of fight or flight. Although the high octane of intense emotion may give you an excuse to avoid taking responsibility for your actions, the Panic Zone is not a place where you want to be.

Once you feel this sense of panic come over you, it's time to step back and reevaluate what you are doing and what led you there.

When my father passed away in July of 2021, I was left with the job of managing his estate. I uprooted my life in Arizona to drive across the country, to a town and a home I hadn't seen before. This was the first time I had ever had to manage an estate, on top of dealing with the death of a parent. There was so much to do, and I had very little knowledge of the area, the house, and the laws governing the process. Talk about being outside of my comfort zone! It was an overwhelming and frightening experience compounded by grief and trying to manage my emotions over the loss of my father.

I took one small step at a time. I went through the paperwork, took inventory of items, spoke with the neighbors, and hired an attorney. It took time and patience. I had to stretch myself into areas where I had little knowledge. I realized I had to ask questions. In the process of doing research, I spent time getting to know the locals, touring the town, and gradually increasing confidence that I could in fact handle this challenge.

Despite these efforts, there were times when I stumbled back into the Risk Zone. Repairs on my father's house were time-consuming and difficult. Roadblocks to getting the paperwork completed popped up, and I felt the strain of doing all of this by myself. Late nights wore me down, and I started to feel overwhelmed, stressed, and anxious.

Before long, I entered the Panic Zone and there was no looking back. I was angry and frustrated that I was left to do all this work. I really just wanted to give up and leave, let someone else pick up the job. I had uprooted my life and been living in Ohio for close to four months at that point. I felt as if I was frozen in time while everyone around me and back in Arizona went about their lives.

Fortunately, I realized that I was in the Panic Zone, and that I had a path out. I took a step back from my emotions, provided myself with some self-care, and reminded myself that everything happens for a reason. I saw this situation as an opportunity to grow and began moving myself back into the Stretch Zone. Things came together: the paperwork was approved, I got access to accounts, made new friends, found an auctioneer, and finished up little tasks. I began to be grateful that even though my father was not there in person, he was there in spirit through his photos, clothing, familiar smells, and personal belongings.

Facing up to this challenge really taught me about my resilience and ability to conquer the unknown. I learned about who I am as a leader, put my coaching skills to the test, and was able to accomplish something I would never have thought I could do just by doing that *1% More!*

Believe it or not, we all have the ability to reach the Stretch Zone!

Further explore where you are currently, and answer the following questions…

What zone are you currently in (Comfort, Stretch, Panic)? And Why?

_____

_____

_____

_____

What is one thing you can do today to move you 1% more outside your comfort zone that can make a change in your life?

_____

_____

_____

_____

How do you manage yourself when you reach the Panic Zone?

CHAPTER 12

_____

_____

_____

_____

THE CYCLE OF INTEGRITY

"Integrity is the ingredient that will enable you to forge rapidly ahead on the highway that leads to success. It advertises you as being an individual who will always come through. Whatever you say you will do, do it even if you have to move heaven and earth."

— *Mary Kay*

There are many ways to grow as a human being. So far, we've looked at the five areas of growth: ***Mental, Social, Spiritual, Emotional,*** and ***Physical.*** These five areas are essential to review on a regular basis to have a proper balance and alignment within your life. We've also explored the three types of zones, ***Comfort, Stretch,*** and ***Panic,*** and how important it is to stretch your limits to achieve growth.

Growth is not an easy process, as babies, we first learn to crawl, then to pull ourselves up, and eventually on to learning how to walk. Each big step along the way is really made of taking small steps, reaching milestones, and doing that *1% More!*

Growing as an individual does come with its challenges. We will be challenged by our friends, our family, and the world around us. We will constantly be tested by unconscious and conscious attempts by others to push us off our pathway. How we act and respond will shape how we grow as individuals and leaders in life.

Ask yourself, *What type of person do I want to be in life? Do I want to be one that person who is known to be reliable and trustworthy? Or, as someone who doesn't keep his or her agreements?*

Integrity is critical to your personal growth. It's about how you show up in life, how you behave publicly and behind closed doors. It's about taking responsibility, being honest, trustworthy, having and following moral principles, and most of all living with energetic wholeness.

Imagine a string of holiday lights that you pulled out of a box. You go and plug it in and see that the lights are only partially working. A bulb is out, causing some of the lights not to work. When one light goes out it causes a disruption in the system which interrupts its full potential and energy. Not until the bulb is replaced will that string of colorful lights radiate again. When your integrity is out of alignment, it interrupts your aliveness and energy.

Integrity is a choice that we make, every day. It is a characteristic that is learned and must be actively practiced. It's about doing the right thing when no one is looking, even when the choice isn't easy to make. Acting with integrity means staying true to yourself and living up to your word!

I want to share a quick family story. As I shared earlier in the book, my uncle has significantly influenced my life. When my brother and I were kids, my mother sent us out to rake the neighbor's leaves. We weren't crazy about the idea, despite the promise of being paid for the work. We went to the neighbor's house and raked the leaves, but we were more interested in getting it done quickly than in doing the job right. Our minds were on other, more important things (like playing video games, of course!). The neighbor paid us but made a phone call to our mother to remark on our poor performance, including not finishing the job.

My uncle heard about the call and decided to talk to me and my brother about what we had done. He talked to us about taking responsibility for our actions, and that when we agree to do something, our *"Word"* is our bond. I remember him saying, *"People make promises all the time, most of them are broken, but your 'word' is your bond, and without that, you have nothing. Your 'word' is how people will judge you and see how you show up in life."*

My brother and I took his words to heart and went back to the neighbor's house the next day to finish raking the leaves. The neighbor was pleased, and we learned the importance of being responsible, accountable, and holding true to our word. Still to this day, many years later, that story has stuck with me. When I look someone in the eye and tell them I am giving them my *"Word"*, they know and can feel the promise behind it.

Ask yourself: How do I show up in life? Am I living with integrity? When I give someone my "Word" do I come through as promised?

Integrity is important in life, not only for itself, but because it means we don't need to spend time questioning our actions or ourselves. We don't need to hide things; we gain the trust of others, are accountable and dependable. When we do the right thing, it makes life simpler.

We are all human, and sometimes we make mistakes. This means we can and do fall out of integrity. We see this dramatically when a prominent figure, politician, or even someone you know loses their integrity through the course of lying, cheating, or stealing, and ends up in a scandal. Many people make decisions based upon their own self-interests, being in the "all about the me" mindset.

For personal growth to happen, we need to hold ourselves to a higher moral standard!

I want to share with you what I call the *Cycle of Integrity*™. I like to think that every day we start fresh and have a choice between coming up with *Reasons* why we've failed or acting in a way that brings *Results.*

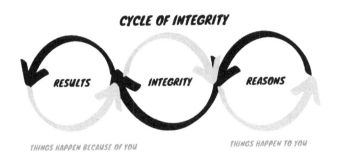

When we live in the world of *Reasons*, we believe things just happen to us. We think we have had no choice in the matter and feel powerless. We start to blame others, create excuses, and wait and hope for something better to happen. When nothing changes, we find more *Reasons* to blame the world and fall deeper and deeper into a *victim mentality.*

On the other hand, when we make the choice to live with integrity, we begin to live a life of *Results!* This is a heart-centered place where things happen because you have made the choice to hold yourself accountable for your actions. By taking ownership of your circumstances, you are in a place to create **Results**. You are self-aware, learning from the experiences, and find that your values, desires, and actions are aligned for success.

It's easy to fall out of integrity throughout our lives. It happens when we make promises to show up on time but don't. It happens when we are asked to follow through on tasks that we then forget about. Maybe we tell a little white lie to stay out of trouble with a partner. Maybe we take shortcuts to finish a project.

Making small concessions like these may seem like no big deal, but eventually, it can begin to snowball into larger issues if we're not paying attention and being careful. I still fall out of integrity occasionally, but I don't allow myself to get trapped there. I recognize my behavior and begin to restore my integrity to myself and to those around me.

Restoring integrity can be a little nerve-racking. Emotions, whether yours or someone else's (or both), often are involved. Regardless, it's important to correct your situation, and use a simple process to help you **R.E.S.T.O.R.E.** ™ your integrity.

1. ***Responsibility*** - Take responsibility! Immediately recognize your wrong behavior and accept full responsibility for it and recognize that you broke your word. Do not allow yourself to see yourself as the victim in the situation.

2. *Eliminate* - Remove any story or narrative that you've created in your head about the situation, all of the "would've, could've, should've" thoughts running through your mind that you use to explain and justify your wrongdoing.

3. *State* - Acknowledge what happened, don't hide from it. State the promise you made, how you broke it, and how breaking it impacted all parties involved.

4. *Truth* - Tell the truth about the situation and share what happened. Keep the story honest, short, and to the point. For example, "I was talking on the phone with a friend and lost track of time."

5. *Ownership* - Take ownership and apologize for what went wrong. Be sincere in your apology. Taking ownership shows is not someone else's responsibility but your own.

6. *Remake* - Remake the promise and clear up the agreement. State what course of action (who, what and by when) you are able to take. It could be something like, "Moving forward, I'll set an alarm 15 mins early so I don't lose track of time."

7. *Engage* - Request feedback and look for other opportunities for growth. Ask if there is something you can do to compensate: "Is there something I can do to make it up to you? Or "How can I restore trust with you?"

Let's take look at integrity in your life, answer the following question below...

Take inventory of your life; in what areas are you currently out of integrity and why?

_____

_____

_____

_____

How will you go about restoring integrity in one or more of these areas?

_____

_____

_____

_____

How would restoring your integrity make that 1% More difference in your life?

_____

_____

_____

_____

When you learn how to become more impeccable with your agreements, you will start to see far less problems and drama in your life. Restoring your integrity leads to getting more things done, less time wasted, and stronger relationships. Living within the world of integrity creates a strong and reliable foundation for a sound life and is a critical element of **Growth**.

As you will see in the following stories from these inspiring individuals there are many ways to grow. They will be sharing about living into your greatness, activating your life, the healing power of a story, becoming a warrior, and much more!

CHAPTER 13

THE SEED OF GREATNESS

By Alexander Richmond

"The true measure of success is also you maintaining who you are by the time you reach the pinnacle of success. Never compromise who you are, or you will become the product of someone else's success. Become the entrepreneur who sells you and don't become the product that's packaged, bought, and sold by others. Will Robins"

— *Delainie Robins*

At a party recently, where I was introduced as a former Olympic wrestler and world champion in Brazilian Jiu-Jitsu, many people came up to me asking questions. One question took me by surprise, yet I had to think about it: What is the seed for your greatness to accomplish such extraordinary successes?

First, I wanted to say things like, "I was hungry for more in life," "I never gave up on my vision," "I had grit," and so on, yet I had to think about it. Although I knew that those were vital contributing factors, I wanted to know: What was the actual seed for all of it? What was that something that made it all possible?

When I was six years old, I began to be trained to the level of a world-class athlete in a sport that I loved. I loved everything about it. From here, my growing-up years was a time of sweat, pain, personal sacrifice, and many tears. Yet, it was all worth the feelings of love I felt for the sport, challenges, and friends & family - everyone who supported me directly or indirectly. I felt joy in every accomplishment along the way, for myself and the team, and in the realization that without them, I could not have come so far.

I cherish the African saying: "If you want to go fast - go alone, but if you want to go far - go with the many!" I knew that going with others was yet another contributing factor but not the seed. I also knew the seed had to be within me and only there. I wondered: Was it a part of my DNA, or is this something everyone has?

After contemplating for a while, I had that aha moment, that insight I was looking for. It is **UNCONDITIONAL LOVE**. Crazy it might sound, follow my thoughts, and see what evidence I found.

There are two types of love: unconditional and conditional love. We are all spiritual beings and part of the whole, the universe with everything in it. We are from the same source for which every human has been gifted the powers of the universe, including unconditional love, no matter what our roles or purposes in life.

Conditional love, on the contrary, is a form of love we adopted after many generations of conditioning through judgments, attachments, and adherence to the rules and standards within our societies and cultures of what is expected of us. This conditioning limits our powers, and we forget who we truly are, spiritual beings, co-creators with extraordinary powers.

In the book Power vs. Force by Dr. David Hawkins, M.D., Ph.D., he analyzes the hidden determinants of human behavior, explaining what humans will experience through measured energy levels. He tells us that the baseline of power is courage, and when we go beyond it, we begin to experience happiness and productivity. As we increase our power and capacity to the levels of love, joy, and peace, we experience synchronicity and extraordinary outcomes.

Dr. Hawkins also demonstrates the impact of force, as force is a less effective energy with guilt and shame on the bottom, leaving us powerless. Meaning conditional love is love drained of some of its power and leaving us less fulfilled in life. Living a life of power means we attract into our lives that which we want. When we have less power, we use force in an attempt to get what we want. Unfortunately, our powers and abilities are hardly used or recognized. When they are seen, those who possess them are seen as extraordinary when, in reality, we are all gifted with them. So, the questioning immediately rises to; how can we accomplish that?

As a child, when I made my decisions, I remembered I didn't always look for evidence or did what seemed to make sense. Instead, I intuitively did whatever I felt was right or what I wanted to do. When I began to wrestle, I loved everything about it: The challenges, the family environment, the toughness, the caring and support, and whatever helped me grow. Having found my passion, I was in love, which gave me grit. My love and passion allowed me to overcome the pain. The love I had helped me persevere where others gave up. Over years of training and personal development, I made personal sacrifices and stayed disciplined where others could not. I was touched, moved, and inspired by many who helped me.

My mentors believed in me and helped me find myself and grow into the best version of myself possible. Yes, there was the occasional doubter and critic, yet I operated at a higher and stronger frequency. I listened to my supporters and felt their sincerity, their honesty, keeping me accountable in a caring and loving way. It's like a feeling of growing wings to fly, determined to take off, and sore like an eagle in the sky.

I had that vision and the will to continue working on my growth, despite what obstacles I would face along the way. I knew I could only become a champion by meeting the best. I always looked for opportunities to act upon. I could never find objective evidence without trial and error. Everything else are only assumptions. I see now that I can access my powers by following the lead of my core values. I have to stay true to myself to find my purpose in life, and for that need to remain within my authenticity.

The core values are our innate guiding principles that dictate our behavior and action. Core values are the essence of who we are. We hold them to be of worth in our life. If we lose that connection, it becomes unclear what we truly value in life. Our love rises with the positive value we give someone or something. It is so powerful that we can accomplish incredible successes as it keeps us engaged, energized, and positively charged with joy to take on all challenges in the way. We gain momentum as we feel the growth.

Having fun and enjoyment in what we are doing is the foundation for everything in any area of our lives to succeed in. However, when we attach conditions to our love, we create barriers that limit our strengths and abilities, especially when we allow others to do this to us. By pleasing others to gain their love and acceptance, we become inauthentic. We lose our integrity and get stuck as compromising ourselves in this way cannot work overtime. Losing integrity, meaning workability - keeps us stuck in our tracks as we give up our power to act to others.

As an athlete, I never gave up any challenge and never made anyone wrong or blamed any circumstances on my failures. I view life as a fun trip on a cruise ship and for sure predetermined its destination. My journey started when I stepped on it. I have time in between, not sure how long, though, yet determined to make the best of it. We all have the power to choose, at free will, what it will be like. I can create my heaven or hell. I can choose to dance, make friends, see a movie, or go into one of their bars to get drunk and start an argument with someone there.

So, I can choose what I want to create or give my powers to someone else to choose for me. I can find my purpose within me and claim my position in this world or do what others want me to do and have to accept the outcomes. With this, I encourage you to look deeper inside yourself to discover the sleeping powers within, bring them to rise, and become extraordinary yourself. Feel what it is like to soar like an eagle and to live full out by practicing unconditional love as an authentic being!

You've got this.

Let's plant those seeds. Answer the following questions...

Are you providing unconditional or conditional love? And if so in what ways?

_____

_____

_____

What are your core values? How do they guide you in life?

_____

_____

_____

What sleeping powers lie dormant inside you? How can you share them with the world?

_____

_____

_____

ABOUT THE AUTHOR

Alexander's life journey has led him to discover his power and purpose through exploring both wisdom and healing. This powerful discovery has opened the door for him to be a resource for others in sharing his trials and tribulations on his personal path to success and freedom.

As a political prisoner, he experienced both physical and mental torture in former communist East Germany, and through that experience, discovered an inner strength and the capacity to forgive. Some call him the Peaceful warrior. He is a former Olympic wrestler, a world-champion in Brazilian Jiu-Jitsu, and a leadership expert.

He is an international trainer, presenter, speaker, and coach with expertise in success, leadership, and NLP, who has traveled the world providing workshops and giving lectures in Asia, Europe and America. His step by step, proven system has people move from stuck to free, and discover their true potential to gain access to what is possible in taking action to create a happy and fulfilled life.

AUTHOR CONTACT INFORMATION

Alexander T. Richmond, *Success and Mindset Coach*
BANKcode™ Certified Trainer
Phone: 1(480) 688-4646
Email: Coach-Alex@gmx.com

CHAPTER 14

LIFE ACTIVATED

by Alicia Thorp

"Every time you are tempted to react in the same old way,
ask yourself if you want to be a prisoner of the past
or a pioneer of the future."

— Deepak Chopra

Hi, my name is Alicia, and I am a recovering people-pleaser. Yes, this was my addiction, and I am here now, proud to be on the other side, as one time, this addictive habit nearly killed me. I often heard that I was too loud, too energetic, too busy, and too active for most of my life. What that boiled down to was that *I* was too much.

At the time, I do not believe the constant negativity was meant to dull my light, but it did. I slowly stopped being creative, carefree, and seeing life as I once used to, as magical. I began questioning everything I did and made sure that everyone around me was ok with the way I acted. I was constantly making sure I had the approval of others. I always wanted to make sure I was making everyone around me "happy." If I didn't, I was afraid that would make people see me as selfish, and I didn't want to be judged.

Hearing that I was "too much" created a deep-rooted belief that I had to please others. Without even knowing it, I brought that false belief right into my young adulthood. Instead of following my path and creating a lifestyle that was in alignment with my truth, I allowed the word of others to dictate the actions I took in my life. I let others tell me what the best job was, what college I should go to, or what kind of items I should be buying instead of truly connecting with what was best for me. I couldn't like what I liked without the fear of judgment from others, and I didn't even know it! This people-pleasing mentality in me grew heavy over the years and shifted my mindset completely.

During my 20's I had friends who didn't serve me, but I was so focused on wanting to be appreciated and a "good friend" that I could not let go of those semi-toxic relationships. I was too worried about their feelings, and like an addiction, I needed that external validation I received from them. It was a habit and a need I had unintentionally created. I never stopped to see what was truly making me happy or what was making me feel whole.

It wasn't until I saw how my people-pleasing put people I loved in harm's way, did I realize what was even happening and what kind of life I unintentionally created for myself. Luckily, even though terrifying at the time, something I disagreed with so much tested me for a few years. I was people-pleasing and getting caught in between physical altercations or verbal arguments that would eventually spiral me down into a web of untruths and speaking someone else's words instead of my own for fear of hurting the feelings of others. I was allowing the toxic traits of others to prey on me and create this person who was aggressive, argumentative, and combative. I developed anxiety, heart palpitations, and panic attacks. I didn't know it at the time, but it was all steaming from needing external validation and living life on other people's terms. I thought this external validation was a standard way of being. I eventually realized I was wrong.

I was asked to get my family to lie about a situation to have a friend look better for what they did, which shook me.

I began to snap out of it.

They didn't need a good friend, they needed someone to step out and put themselves in a bad situation, and they were asking me to be that person and bring my family into it. I was not ok with that, and I knew I could break out of this vicious cycle of people-pleasing.

I faced a turning point in my life.

How did I get here? I was going through a divorce, becoming a single mom who couldn't afford much more than my car payment, and I was living off food stamps. Others judged me, and I felt a stabbing pain in my gut, as I would never have judged anyone, and here I was being judged. I came to the harsh realization that people-pleasing got me nowhere and that it wasn't up to me to make everyone else feel good before me. It was about me.

It was time for me to activate my life.

I chose to begin creating MY life and showing up for ME first. I set boundaries, found the power in saying "no" to others was saying "yes" to me, and I began taking aligned action.

I knew that it would take more than just a positive thought to change my lifestyle. It had to be an entire mindset shift, and it was time I got activated. There was more for me than people-pleasing and pushing my passions under the rug. I was ready to emerge and stop living my life reacting to other people.

I began to align myself with my passions and committed to living in my purpose. I believed with everything I had that I was meant for more. I visualized what I wanted. I began to accept what I wanted. I stopped chasing the external validation I was receiving from others. I could get that myself by following my truth and my passions. I needed to praise myself and maximize my strengths internally. I started to have expectations for myself and my life, and I was dreaming big. I was becoming an active participant in my life, no longer accepting standing on the sidelines and waiting for the approval of others to play the game of my life.

I became a yoga instructor in 2016 to get an even more profound connection with my true self and began practicing mindset in 2018. I started coaching, creating courses and programs to assist others. I found coaches doing what I wanted to be doing, and I began learning from them. I started showing up authentically. I became the damn expert in my life.

Within a few short years, I did it. I created the life of MY dreams. I had the dream husband, the dream job, the dream house, the dream family. I didn't allow anyone to stop me from showing up as that better and aligned version of myself. I bought the luxury bags and name-brand shoes because they made me feel good. I knew purchasing items that I truly wanted was never to show off for someone but to show up for me, and that felt good.

I showed appreciation daily for my past, and I share gratitude daily today.

I am currently a multi-passionate, successful mom, wife, and business owner. I am a leader in my direct sales company, a Spiritual and Yoga Mindset Coach, working a 9-5, raising three beautiful children with my soul mate husband in my dream home.

Even if I was uncertain, saying "yes" to me was the best course of action I ever took. I invite you to become the most excellent version of yourself too. It is within us all to be, do, and have greatness from within.

Activate your life today! Answer the following questions...

Are you a people pleaser? If so, in what ways? How can you put a stop to it?

_____

_____

_____

_____

How can you begin to activate your life? What actions can you take?

_____

_____

_____

_____

What would it look like if you were able to align your vision, passion and purpose?

_____

_____

_____

_____

ABOUT THE AUTHOR

Alicia Thorp is a mother, wife, yoga instructor and Mindfulness Practitioner. Alicia believes in the power of self-love, self-care, and gratitude. These powerful tools helped her to live the lifestyle she knew she was meant for. A life that at one time she could only dream of.

Alicia learned the power of mindset when she was going through a very difficult time in her life. She became a yoga instructor, got certifications in reiki and natural healing as well as her certification in mindfulness. In 2017 Alicia began to help guide other women to live with more clarity in order to keep achieving what they desired, without hesitation, in both their professional and personal life.

Alicia is a two-time Amazon Best Selling Author, has spoken on stages and has coached women on Mindfulness, Spiritual Healing and deepening their connection to living the life they desire.

You have the power to change your future, Alicia is your Mentor along your journey.

AUTHOR CONTACT INFORMATION

Alicia Thorp, *Yoga Instructor and Mindfulness Practitioner*
Email: Mentor.AliciaThorp@gmail.com

CHAPTER 15

MULTI-DIMENSIONAL REALITY

by Teresa Martell

*"Raising our consciousness from fear to love,
becomes a journey of self-expression and courage."*

— Teresa Martel

*I*magine that we are in a multi-dimensional reality right now. Many have heard this expression but never stop to think what that means to them.

Since 2012, we have been feeling a significant change in our lives and in our surroundings. Imagine that the Earth Shifted during this 2012 phenomenon… Many of those who were awakening prior to 2012 understood it… if not fully, they felt it within their own personal growth into the collective consciousness.

So, what does multi-dimensional reality mean?

Keep in mind, there are others who may explain this phenomenon differently, yet it all means the same thing. It's how we interpret the divine thoughts through our ***Ego Mind***.

There are three dimensions on Earth this very moment leading us into the Awakening of the New Age, and we are living within them. The 3rd Dimension (3D) is the *Fear* based world of acting out our negative emotions: Fear, hate, anger resentment, judgment, anxiety, and depression.

The 4th Dimension (4D) is the now moment, the present, having a knowing about the outer world. Otherwise, the Observer.

The 5th Dimension (5D) is the Collective consciousness and the Christ consciousness of Unconditional Love.

If you are living in a 3D state of consciousness, it would be exceedingly difficult for you to fathom that there is any such reality of 4D and 5D. You would be so attached to your fear-based world and driven by the influence of the world around you, that you would have a hard time grasping the concept. This is thousands of years of conditioning. Fears relate to the wars, the ownership of property, the programming of political and religious rule and following a system that is broken. This is a paradigm of struggle and strife over survival. Money is hard to come by. You work hard to get the things you want. Feeling powerless by allowing the outside world to rule your everyday life.

Individuals shifting into a 4D consciousness are those who have awakened to the reality that there is something more or better than the chaotic lives they had or have been living every day. They are more aware of Self and have begun the healing process of the programmed fears that have burdened them in the 3D. They examine their fearful thoughts and situations and begin the process of observing and putting action in their own lives to see beyond the negative emotions and developing a knowing about what they see of the ever so gloomy programming of the news and the mind control of Political and Religious beliefs system. They realize that those who are suffering are living out their own story. They are becoming an observer and not judging or owning the outside realities of programming. In this state of consciousness, you begin to pay more attention to your inner self and doing the work to change. You begin to become more conscious of your environment and decide what is good for you and what isn't. This is a consciousness that awakens to the magic of becoming the creator of your own world. You begin to understand intuition and begin to see your world begins to revolve around synchronicity and curiosity. You begin to become more of a participant in creating a better future for yourself and assist and be more supportive to others growth as well and be in service.

The 5D consciousness is the reality of Christ like embodiment. It is a spiritual awareness of collective thought. We begin to become aware that we are all energy, and you see that the Universe is always supporting you and your life unfolds as an adventure and life unfolds as into a beauty that you never knew existed before. It goes beyond the 4D but has similar traits as you fluctuate between these two realities by doing the work such as meditating, journaling, discovering that even something bad has good within it. We become enlightened creators looking to work together with a common cause of growth and seeing the Earth as one with all. This consciousness is expansive and can open the doors of a new species of humanity on Earth. There is a kinder approach of like mindedness of living out lighter emotions of Peace, Love, Kindness, Compassion, Happiness and many thoughts and behaviors of positive energies.

To put this all together. We live all of these consciousnesses simultaneously every day. Simple example: You may start your day out quiet, peacefully listening to music while you eat breakfast and get ready for work, (4D.) You go to work, and you overhear someone talking about another employee that is unable to complete his/her job correctly. The person existing in the 4D, would be just observing this conversation with no judgment, or thought about it. A person existing in the 3D consciousness, would be getting in on the conversation and being a part of the gossip. Imagine, you go to work, and that employee comes to you and tells you that she/he is having a difficult time figuring out a certain part of his/her job. You get up and assist that person in learning their particular problem and help that person find a way to remember it for the future.

This 4D action of being in the present moment and not grumbling but assisting in a helpful way is demonstrated through the act of supporting the co-worker. Making that person feel like he/she is part of the working family, being gracious to the person with a smile, and offering to help out again until she/he gets more comfortable in their work is that (5D) connection.

Another example, your teenage son comes home in a rant over a situation from school. You automatically want to help him out, but he takes it out on you with harsh words and slams his bedroom door. In the 3D mindset, you get mad and start yelling at him and accuse him of starting the problem, thus allowing yourself to get all worked up emotionally over his behavior. In the 4D mindset, you begin to calm down and take yourself to a place of understanding, remembering yourself as a teenager with hormones raging, and out of control behavior. You chuckle to yourself; you get centered, you allow him his space. When he comes out of his room to eat dinner, you cheerfully start a conversation at the table about anything other than his behavior. This action raises the vibration to a communal gathering at the kitchen table (5D) allowing him to feel safe to be himself.

It is important to understand that as we evolve, we can live out experiences in the 3D world, because we live in a 3D body. To make money, get married, raise children, become part of a community interest, go to church. To be in 4D is to work through your fear-based emotions and healing them, that raises you into a more compassionate and forgiving nature and opens doors for spirit to move more deeply into your heart.

These are fascinating times. As more people awaken to these concepts of Spiritual Growth, we will surely be bringing forward a New Age of Consciousness as we close the door to the 3D we begin to create our realities in the pathway of how we perceive the God within us. Creating Heaven on Earth. Imagine that!

Multidimensional reality is all around us, answer the following questions…

How are you currently living in the third-dimension world? (fear-based)

_____

_____

_____

_____

How are you currently living in the fourth-dimension world? (the now)

_____

_____

_____

_____

How are you currently living in the fifth-dimension world? (providing unconditional love)

_____

_____

_____

_____

ABOUT THE AUTHOR

*E*ach one of us has a natural, innate ability to maintain and improve our Health and Emotional/Mental well-being.

Teri is a Holistic Practitioner who teaches the Mind, Body, and Spiritual approach of Wellness. She assists the public by using Hypnosis, Reiki (hands on healing), and Astrology as part of her practice.

She has been teaching and certifying a 100-hour course provided by the National Guild of Hypnotists since 1996. She has been in practice for 30 years and continues to teach and mentor individuals to "Invest in Yourself", Physically, Emotionally, Mentally and Spiritually.

AUTHOR CONTACT INFORMATION

Teri Martell, *Holistic Practitioner and Hypnotherapist*
Email: secretsofhealing@yahoo.com
Website: http://secretsofhealing111.com

CHAPTER 16

THE EPIPHANY

By Craig Darling

*"There's nothing better when something comes
and hits you and you think 'YES'!"*

— *J.K. Rowling*

The bright lights and dotted tiles were all I could see aside from the hooks, bags, lines, and the masked faces of those that wheeled me into the operating room. I remember hearing, "You'll have to move from the gurney to the operating table and then count backward from ten."

I felt fear. And I felt — regret?

A week earlier.

"What is this?" my wife Suzette was holding up a large (very large) bottle of migraine pills.

I had purchased two bottles from Costco as I'd been battling a serious headache for months. I was tired of running out of the only thing that would make it stop, so I bought two of the super-sized bottles. I put the large bottle on my nightstand, where it was convenient. Suzette was having none of it. She pressed on and insisted I see someone.

The next day I was waiting for David, a friend and doctor, to see me. All I wanted to do was get back to the office. I was in sales and had deals to close to keep the wolves from the door. David brought me in, he had heard from my wife the reason that I was in his office. We left his office, I dropped Suzette off at home and continued on to work, after all, I needed to get some sales going.

Just as I walked into the office, the phone started ringing. It was David, I needed to get a CAT scan.

"Okay, I'll do it. Who do I call for an appointment?"

"They are waiting for you right now," he replied.

So, I headed back to my car and to the CAT scan so I could return to my office.

Again, I returned to my office to the sound of a ringing phone.

It was David.

"You need to return to the medical center and have an MRI. Two of them. With and without the contrast. Right now. They are waiting for you."

Jeeze, I thought. Am I ever going to get any work done?

Being in that noisy tube for 45 minutes, for two procedures, was unsettling. When I was done, I drove back to my office, determined to rescue the day.

The phone was ringing when I walked into my office — again. My friend, client, and my doctor gave me more news: I had to meet with a neurosurgeon immediately.

I called my wife, we then headed over together for a trip to meet my destiny.

It was strange, that visit. The surgeon was a nice man and smart, thank goodness. It was, after all, brain surgery they were talking about. It seems as if a glioblastoma multiforme tumor (mass the size of a golf ball) was pushing on the ventricle of the brain and it needed to come out. The surgery had risks. Recovery was uncertain, walking and talking were in jeopardy.

I'll admit, I was afraid. I hadn't done anything yet. I was married and had a career, but I didn't have grandchildren yet, I didn't have anything for my wife to carry on with. Walking and talking was how I made a living. The business I had dreamed of building, wasn't.

My eyes opened. I could see the fluorescent lights above my bed. I couldn't move. I was trussed up — immobile. I was also in severe pain. I looked around the room, my eyes being the only thing that I could move, my wife immediately notified the nurse I was awake.

The nurse attended to me, and the surgeon was there shortly after. I was to remain immobile for 24 hours. I didn't yet know if I could walk or talk. The pain was — immense. I couldn't take any type of pain or acid relief (the steroids to keep the brain from swelling turn on the acid pumps in the stomach). They couldn't risk masking any symptoms.

The pain and the discomfort that I experienced over the next 24 hours changed me. As I was going under, I decided that I should start to live. My only relief from the pain was thinking how, exactly, I was going to live.

I was fortunate. I was unwrapped the next day. I could see without my glasses! (that lasted for a week) I could sort of walk. I could sort of talk. People that I love came to see me.

I was home after a few days. I couldn't drive or work, but I could plan and dream and dream and plan. I wrote my business plan. This was all a sort of desperation to achieve something, and I cherished every minute. When interacting with friends and family, I now looked at things in a new light. I now understood that each moment was precious. Every word from a loved one should be treasured. I needed to be true to myself, not a character that I played in this life.

The real recovery started when I wrote a set of goals:

- Share my expertise with businesses that don't have access to my knowledge.
- Spend more time with friends and family.
- Create a business that serves as many people as possible.
- Ensure exceptional continuation of life for my wife and family if anything should happen to me.
- Support and engage in my community to make life, for all of us, better.

Motivated by an epiphany that life was better than what it was, I started pursuing these goals.

Fast forward to today: I've accomplished these goals and am pursuing some even loftier ones today. Even better? I am helping people everywhere to build simple agencies like mine and find prosperity for their families and communities as well.

In goals to make our communities better: I've supplied this expertise to non-profits and supported animal rescue operations whenever possible.

I now serve small businesses in over 20 countries around the world, in 35 States, and growing. I provide core techniques to the world — perhaps, people like you — for free. Anyone can use these techniques to leverage their businesses' visibility. I get amazing amounts of referrals, which fuels my ability to help in even more ways as our company grows.

Seriously, so much has happened since I woke up. And there is still so much to do. Living in Chandler with my wife, three dogs, and two cats, we love to spend time in our garden or visiting locally with our two grandchildren. Life is good... Out of tragedy, came bounty. I embraced it.

Thank you for reading. I'll leave you with one amazing secret about using the internet for your prosperity: You don't need a website anymore.

Feel free to connect with me.

Let's explore epiphanies and answer the following questions...

What areas of your life have your eyes been close to that need to be reopened?

_____

_____

_____

_____

What can you do right now to address these areas to make a 1% More difference?

_____

_____

_____

_____

What would life be like for you, having a new perspective?

_____

_____

_____

_____

ABOUT THE AUTHOR

Craig Darling is a chaser of dreams. He is a Chevrolet Hall of Fame member, SCCA Men's Rookie of the Year 1997.

He was an early Adopter of internet marketing, contributing author, Co-Founder of AdZoo Marketing and Social Outbreak companies and is currently President and CEO of Darling Companies, LLC A GMB Agency with active clients around the globe, delivering management and training services focused on Google My Business and Google tools. The least expensive, most effective, way to be found on the internet today.

AUTHOR CONTACT INFORMATION

Craig Darling, *Google Business Profile Master and Coach*
Website: www.DarlingCompanies.com
Schedule a Face-to-Face appointment: https://bit.ly/3A6r0E8

CHAPTER 17

THE ART OF BEING YOU!

By Corryn Kivett

*"It takes courage to change
and follow your dreams,
courage you have"*

— Corryn Kivett

Ever since I can remember, all I ever wanted to do was make a difference. To help others, make an impact even though I had no idea what that meant.

In 2018, I took a real hard look at my life, and from the outside in it looked like I had it all. I was creating the life I thought I wanted while on the inside I was numb, disconnected, and stagnant - going through the motions, living on autopilot.

Don't get me wrong; I achieved what a lot of people would consider "success." I graduated top of my class from a great college, became a Certified Financial Planner, and moved on to be a Financial Advisor for one of the top wealth management firms in the U.S at the age of 25. The ability to set a goal, achieve it, and move on to the next is natural for me because it's the environment I grew up in.

My upbringing trained me to consistently be in the pursuit of achieving success and accepting nothing less than my best. Reality is achieving success has always been easy, however, I ended up doing it for all the wrong reasons and internally struggled in the process.

Some might look at me and think I grew up having it all when just like everyone else, I've learned how to play the cards I was dealt. I'll refrain from going into detail of what it was like being raised by a single mom running her own business and a dad who was there one day and gone the next – let's just say it made me a stronger person. Truth be told, I was constantly looking for approval in everything I did to prove I was good enough for my dad to stay.

 I excelled in school, straight A's, trained exceptionally hard in sports - basketball and volleyball since I had the height – doing everything I knew to do, yet none of it seemed good enough.

Everything shifted at the age of 13. My dad wanted a better relationship between the two of us so that's what we started to build. Those few months I'll never forget - I thought it was going to be a new life between us until suddenly something happened out of my control. He became terminally ill with Stage 4 cancer in a very short time and passed away before I could say goodbye.

To say it was a shock to my mind, body, and spirit is an understatement. I turned to what I knew best: set goals, achieve them, and keep moving forward. Acting as if everything was fine and putting all of my energy into achieving. Climbing the corporate ladder, getting designation after designation, and chasing money while continuing to seek approval and acknowledgment from the outside world.

I unknowingly created a life built out of a house of cards, a weak foundation based on approval from others, opinions, fear of the unknown, and tying my self-worth to my career.

Shakespeare says, "To thine own self be true," and the reality was, I didn't know myself.

I was choosing to live a life incongruent to who I truly was; pretending to enjoy a career I hated; wearing the clothes I thought I was supposed to wear, worrying about what others thought of me while criticizing and judging myself non-stop.

Against everything I was told, I left the corporate career with zero plan and hit what most saw as "rock bottom." Battling anxiety, struggling financially, and worrying about what I had just done with my life, I fell into "waiting mode." Waiting for someone to save me and tell me what to do. The reality is the only person who is going to get me to where I want to go is the person staring back at me in the mirror.

Where we go, we follow, and I knew that for me to get somewhere I had never been I needed to become someone I had never been. I tripped over Neuro-Linguistics Programming, which at the time was a very big word I knew nothing about - all I knew was I wanted to get out of my way and build the business and life I actually wanted. I reluctantly chose to invest in my personal and professional development, so I could see my blind spots, learn from them, and evolve. I say reluctantly because I had never invested in myself and the thought of investing money in my development was a lot to swallow, especially when I was making less than $250 a month.

I started peeling back the programs of self-judgment, doubt, lacking money mindset, and perfectionism, and leaned into trusting, believing, and valuing myself while taking new actions. I decided to become a certified Neuro-Linguistics Programming Master Coach and Trainer then launched the Evolution Room, a coaching and training company, which I have successfully continued to build. In less than 24 months I went from making $250 a month to selling in a single day what I made annually in the corporate world.

I've learned that to be the true artist of our lives, we must first uncover who we really are by reawakening the dreamer within us; the part of us that knows the path to our authentic success yet has been shoved into a corner, put aside, and told to stay quiet.

See, the moment we are born, we come into this world as a blank slate, nothing but pure possibility. We are fully alive in the joy of dreaming and then life happens. We slowly begin to shape ourselves to the world around us, shifting our wants and dreams based on the cards we are dealt.

Our focus moves away from the dream of what could be, to what other people think or say is *possible* for us. Shaping our vision based on this *reality*, unknowingly putting ourselves in a box and accepting it as truth.

Going through the motions, covering up that dream with the burden of all that we are supposed to do, who we are supposed to be, what we are supposed to want and how we are supposed to act.

The heart of true authentic success, whatever the definition is, requires us to peel back the mask we've been trained to wear so we can listen to the part of us that knows who we really are, what we truly want and how to make it happen.

When we come from this place, *success is simple.*

Now, I get to fulfill my deepest desire to make a difference and help business owners create the business and life they truly desire. So many people talk about being in your purpose and now I finally get what they mean.

No matter where you are, no matter what you're going through, this can be your day one. My wish for you is that you continue to evolve, peel back the layers of what you think, or feel is possible and arrive at what has been patiently waiting for you all along.

Embrace the art of being you because it's the key to your success.

Let's explore the power of being you! Answer the following questions...

Are you building your foundation on a house of cards? What areas of your life are not as strong as they should be?

_____

_____

_____

_____

Is your life aligned with who you are now?

_____

_____

_____

_____

What layers do you need to peel away to be your true authentic self to find happiness?

_____

_____

_____

_____

About The Author

Most people settle and call it "making a living." High-Performance Coach Corryn Kivett believes there's a better way to live. There is a science behind becoming a powerful leader and it begins with getting out of your own way.

Corryn is the founder of Evolution Room, the place where business owners transform their business and bank accounts. As a Master Coach and Trainer in Neuro-Linguistics Programming and High Performance, she equips leaders and entrepreneurs with functional tools and resources to effectively communicate, successfully sell and master their mindset through proven scientific strategies. She's driven to empower leaders to get unstuck, create breakthroughs and thrive in any environment by starting with the end in mind.

Corryn teaches others how to get on the path of financial success and purpose. Her own path began after working as a financial planner at one of the largest Wealth Management Firms in America. Raised by two entrepreneurs, Corryn was taught to pursue stability, which meant a 9 to 5 job in corporate America. So, she attended a university and graduated with honors with a bachelor's in business administration (finance emphasis), then landed a dream job working as a financial planner at Merrill Lynch in San Diego. Although successful, it wasn't for her. She realized she was chasing someone else's dream and needed to follow her own. In 2018 she finally listened to her intuition, which told her to follow her passion into personal development.

Corryn became an NLP Master Coach and Trainer, then launched Evolution Room to help visionaries, change makers and entrepreneurs create a purposeful existence and perform at their optimal level. As an experienced and knowledgeable guide, she helps clients transform their personal and professional lives, giving them the courage to evolve into their full potential.

AUTHOR CONTACT INFORMATION

Corryn Kivett, *High Performance Coach*
Website - https://evolutionroom.co/
Email: corryn@evolutionroom.co
Phone: 619-333-6742
IG: @corrynkivett
Linkedin: https://linkedin.com/in/corryn-kivett-12800364

CHAPTER 18

THE HEALING POWER OF STORY

By Becky Norwood

"Storytelling brings to light untapped wisdom,
heals lives, and transforms hearts. It is a path for growth
and sharing. And LIVING!"

— Becky Norwood

For far too many years, my voice was silent. As a child, the words I heard were, "You are ugly, you are stupid, and you will never make it in the world." As I grew into adulthood, I felt unworthy and almost powerless as I struggled to make sense of life. Yet, buried deeply under the surface was something calling me. A deep knowing, yearning, and feeling that there was some- thing more kept calling me. And I began to listen.

With time, with listening to the still and quiet voice deep within, and with reaching out to others who were leading the way, I discovered my gifts and began honing those gifts in a way that certainly made my own life richer, more complete, and certainly much happier. In the process, I discovered my calling. I discovered how I would serve the world as a leader.

I discovered that life had prepared me with unique experiences, well-earned wisdom, creative talents, and treasured gifts. I have learned that the only real failure in life is the failure to grow from what we have gone through.

In conversations with so many women, I find an overriding theme that plagues so many of us. I have observed that theme to be self-worth. So many women speak about feeling unworthy or having struggled with feelings of unworthiness.

I came from an excessively abusive background as a child. It was filled with abuse that occurred daily, not only for myself but for my mother and siblings. Countless stories of my childhood and young adulthood are tough to share, but it was in the sharing of those stories that I found myself.

In my youth, hiding the truth was painstakingly drilled into my psyche. The fear of exposing the truth and losing my life for doing so was very real. Mix that with the required, "telling the truth" of every conversation, be it with classmates, teachers, or adults – in minute detail, to an obsessive, mean-spirited, abusive father who was paranoid that his true colors would be exposed, and you have the resulting pain, confusion, and disillusionment of the victims.

As I stepped into adulthood, I was utterly conflicted, confused, and certainly on a path to attract all the good my heart desired. Indeed, my healing journey has not been on a straight path, it has taken many twists and turns, and I suspect it will continue to do so.

I became a single mom when I was six months pregnant with my second baby. The oldest of the two was just 13 months old. I had married a man who was just like my father. However, having my children was the catalyst to the awakening that there was more to life than what had gone before, and I was determined that my children would have a beautiful life.

I began reading and searching for something… and that something developed into an opportunity to attend a week-long power of thought school. That week my heart was open, and my mind was exposed to incredible new ways of thinking. Bolstered, excited, and inspired, I returned home with a newfound awareness of my self-worth, my inner strength, and goodness.

After returning from my trip, I went to my father's home and asked him to join me on the patio for a conversation.

During that conversation, I told him how his abuse had affected me, and that while I was no longer under his roof, his abuse had left an indelible mark. I reminded him that he was still abusing my mother. Much was said that fateful evening. As we spoke, he became increasingly hostile and angry. Finally, I told him that it was time for him to leave. He could pack up his belongings, take what money he needed, take his jeep and camp trailer, and go find his happiness. I told him how sorry I was that none of his family had brought him joy, but it was time for this to end. I told him I would seek out protection for myself, my daughters, and my mother if he chose not to leave peacefully.

He was not a happy camper.

A few days later he knocked on my door saying he needed to speak with me. I was reluctant to talk, even more so to let him into my home. I stepped outside, fearful of what he was going to say.

These were his words, "Becky, I am so proud of you."

Shocked by his words, I asked why he would say such a thing. He responded, "Look what you have done. You have broken the pattern of abuse that has happened for generations of our family.

Look at the way you are raising your children. You are good to them, you treat them with respect, and discipline with kindness.

Look at what remarkable young women they have become."

As I stood dumbfounded and in tears, I said, "Dad, abuse does not work. It does not produce goodness." He said, "I know. You have taught me that." That was his greatest gift.

Three weeks later, he did leave, but with none of his belongings. That night, he did not return to his home. The next morning, I went to the sheriff and reported him missing. For the first time in my life, I shared my story. The Sheriff, who sat in disbelief, questioned, and double questioned. He knew my father, knew he was a difficult man, had even served on the City Council with him, but had not known the full scope of just how difficult he was. I requested that my mom and daughters and I have witness protection. Although I suspected what he had done, I could not be sure, and his repeated threats kept haunting me. I also begged the Sheriff not to make public the fact that he was missing because of my being in so much fear of the repercussions.

Two weeks later, the Sheriff insisted that it had to be broadcast on the news, and though they had searched to no avail… they could not wait any longer. I consented, and just hours after it was broadcast, someone reported having seen his vehicle about 50 miles out on a remote area of the desert.

He had taken his life the day he left.

Initially, I blamed myself for his death, even though I knew that it was a blessing for our family. He had come from a family of horrible abuse, and I was aware of his pain-filled childhood and the atrocities he had gone through.

His pain was also now over, and so was the deep pain our family experienced.

Fast Forward…

In time, I found that buried deep within me was the fire that prompted that four-year-old to attempt escape. And it was that fire that has also led me to the healing that continues and the work I now do in helping others discover the healing power of story.

The biggest step I took in my healing was writing and publishing my book, "The Woman I Love." That woman was ME! For a fact, until I could love myself, all the dreams, wishes, and desires I held in my heart would not come to me. What transpired from publishing my book which became a #1 international bestseller is that it paved the way to the discovery of my life's work.

In essence, my story became the gateway for conscious growth, a pathway for sharing, and brought healing for myself and others. It became the thread that has woven the tapestry that would lead me to become an advocate for courageousness and the freedom that sharing our stories brings. It became the discovery of my treasured gifts and my life's work.

Writing my own book and sharing my story in a book was only the beginning. It was when I began working with my private clients that I saw the true transformational power that lies in storytelling.

Now, as I work with authors to tap into the incredible power that emerges from storytelling, I am humbled daily by the stories I hear. It brings me such deep joy to witness others showing up in the world with raw vulnerability sharing their stories.

Just as I had experienced, by saying YES to sharing the painful stories of our past we discover special gifts we never knew existed.

In my case, accepting my own story allowed me to release the story, to let it go, and no longer hold power over me. It opened the door to possibilities beyond my wildest imagination. In time, I learned that owning my story would actually amplify the special gifts I had no idea I possessed. My own sordid, painful stories lead me to discover my life's purpose.

As I work with authors to craft the words of their life's journey, I am constantly reminded that I did not hold a corner on the market for troubled times. What a delight to work with so many from incredibly different backgrounds who have withstood incredibly tough situations. They have found their way and now serve as teachers and leaders in our world, standing up, sharing their stories, their wisdom, and their expertise. There is not one of us who can escape life on this planet without earth-shattering events that rock our world.

Storytelling can bring to light untapped wisdom.
Storytelling can heal lives.
Storytelling can transform the heart.
Story is the gateway for growth.
It's a path for sharing.
Story is what brings us closer to one another.
And it's through the threads of our
stories that we weave together an empowered new world.

After publishing my story, and I began to witness working with others, I became deeply aware of the powerful and deeper impact storytelling can have. I discovered the amplification of storytelling skills. Its intrinsic value lends itself to becoming advocates, truth tellers, unifiers, and way-showers.

Stories are up to 22 times more memorable than facts alone and help others see a new way of viewing life. Developed and used purposefully, I advocate using storytelling to reach hearts, which contributes to inclusion and connection, building confidence, and bringing about change.

Storytelling is how we interact with each other about values; how we share experiences, counsel each other, comfort each other, and inspire each other to action. By incorporating the story of self, the story of us, and the story of now, we can create a new public narrative. This is advocacy in its purest form!

So, I ask you...

- How would telling your story move and inspire others?
- What would sharing your story do for you?
- How can you break free of any resistance to telling your story?
- In what ways could that freedom bless you?
- In what ways could it bless others?

The greatest gift we can give ourselves is to love ourselves. The greatest gift we can give our families is to love ourselves. The greatest gift we can give the world is to love ourselves.

We do not owe our past a place in our future.

> *"The irony is that we attempt to dis-own our difficult stories to appear more whole or more acceptable. But our wholeness, even our wholeheartedness depends on the integration of all of our experiences, including the falls."*
> *- Brené Brown*

Our stories are our connectors, and as such, a well-told story can have a huge impact on transformational change in others.

How can you begin to create a new story?

Regardless of where your story begins, know that you have a story to tell. A story filled with treasured gifts that the world is waiting to experience… by telling it you will find you have a story well-told.

We all have a story within. Answer the following questions…

How would telling your story move and inspire others? What would sharing your story do for you?

_____

_____

_____

_____

How can you break free of any resistance to telling your story?

_____

_____

_____

_____

In what ways could that freedom bless you? In what ways could it bless others?

_____

_____

_____

_____

ABOUT THE AUTHOR

#1 International Bestselling author, speaker, & book publishing expert, Becky Norwood is CEO of Spotlight Publishing™. She is widely recognized for the empowering 'story whisperer' intuitive way she passionately guides others to become their very own story whisperer. She incorporates her methods with sound marketing which is the pathway for business expansion and audience growth.

Becky has brought over 350 authors to #1 best-seller. Countless listeners have heard her live online interviews of both authors and experts offering sage advice. She offers an extensive catalog of services supporting emerging and established authors.

The LIGHT in Spotlight means:

Loving Influencers Growing Heartfelt Transformations

Those are the authors we serve!

AUTHOR CONTACT INFORMATION

Becky Norwood - *CEO Spotlight Publishing, Book Publishing Expert*
Website: https://www.spotlight-publishing.pro
Email: support@spotlightpublishing.pro
Facebook: https://www.facebook.com/SpotlightBookPublishing
LinkedIn: https://www.linkedin.com/in/beckybnorwood/

CHAPTER 19

GROWING BEYOND LIMITATIONS

By Christopher Shiver

"There are no limitations to the mind
except those we acknowledge."

— Napoleon Hill

"Mind over matter" is an iconic, over-used platitude found in today's society; it's also the least understood. The saying makes me think of individuals like Bruce Lee, Gandhi, and Goku, and of some of the most famous motivational speeches. The concept is one of the most used Hollywood drama tropes out there. But the message is the same–with enough willpower any obstacle can be overcome.

Like many other people, I used the idea to jump-start my journey of self-development. And like many others, after enough time passed, I realized that I had begun to experience a plateau in my growth. I experienced months where I regressed and found myself unable to maintain the same level of enthusiasm and growth.

I want you to understand that "mind over matter" is a great way to get started. But leaning on it too much will eventually stunt your growth. The expression makes for great training wheels but will keep you from going faster if you continue to rely on it. It's easy to fall into the willpower trap, hence it's important that you step back and actually reflect on your journey. When I reflected on my journey, I realized that willpower is not enough. To surpass and grow past myself, I had to grasp the concept of a growth mindset.

It's not easy to truly get the depth of this concept because every individual has to find his or her own path to develop the ability to grow past their limitations. Getting the best out of a growth mindset is entirely dependent on a person's ability to create concrete and measurable goals. The ability to establish specific goals is critical, because the truth of the matter is your brain is your greatest enemy, an enemy that doesn't want you to change for the better and finds ways to knock you off the path you've set for yourself. Clear and measurable goals keep you accountable and most of all provide clarity on how goals are affecting you. With new understanding, I adopted several beliefs like this saying from NLP, "there is no such thing as failure, only feedback." Incorporating these beliefs into my identity from the "mind over matter" platitude I started with, gave me the opportunity to grow outside of the edges of my metaphorical box.

Before making this change in my mindset, I had just dropped out of the University of Arizona and had reached the worst level of depression in my life. I had begun to inflict shame on myself for what at the time seemed an obvious fact: that my mind was not stronger than my body. I was experiencing failures and attributing them to mental weakness. Luckily for me, through my mentorship, I learned that the mental states we find ourselves in are built out of the frames and perceptions of the present moment. Without knowing it, I had led myself into creating the belief that I could not get my life together because of my lack of willpower. I soon learned that holding tightly onto the "mind over matter" concept had pushed me into a corner. Sadly, many people find themselves in this corner, where they beat themselves up for their failures and wonder why they can't get out.

My euphoria at freeing myself from my self-imposed mental prison was the most gratifying feeling I had ever experienced. I was enthusiastic about the level of growth now open to me. I prioritized cultivating my social dexterity and physical exercise and stepped into the world of entrepreneurship. My growth was literally exponential– from a quiet shut-in to a socialite. I discovered a love for talking to people. Opening myself up to strangers brought lots of opportunities and especially changed my life.

Getting outside my comfort zone taught me to appreciate the value of making an effort and persevering through difficulty. Just another example of the power perspective can have over behavior. I actually relished challenges and found myself appreciating my failures more than my success. I started an export and import business that became my main source of income in my twenties and although I had some failures along the way, they did not deter me as they have in the past.

I am not perfect, and I still have blind spots. There are parts of my life that could use the growth mindset. The ego has this amazing ability to keep the things we are most scared of tackling out of our sight. With reflection, I've found these blind spots and am working on using the growth mindset to overcome them. It's the toughest thing anyone can do because we have spent our entire lives avoiding them and confronting those areas can be difficult. But after the hard-fought battle, win or lose, the new realizations we have gained are the most soul-shattering moments that open room for massive transformation.

Isn't that what it's all about? We want that moment when we know we will never be the same again. We have changed for the better. The moment of transformation is the best part of every story and movie out there, or the athlete's life that we follow.

I am now a father and provider for my family and that brings new territory for me to explore. I'm finding other blind spots as I learn about myself in those new environments. Fortunately, I have found that using the growth mindset in one field has led to improved skills in other areas. I am more confident in what I want to do with my life and see a plethora of opportunities.

Gone are the days when I would just give up when things got tough, no more creating my own self-imposed prison by telling myself things that lead me to defeat. I have realized that failing, even being bad at something, is initially and simply a choice someone must make. Yeah, I may not be good at this task right now, but I can get better, I can always get better. I hope my children inherit this way of being.

Let's begin going beyond our limits, take action and answer the following questions…

What goals would you like to achieve in the next 1, 3, 5, 7, 10, 20 years from now?

_____

_____

_____

_____

How would looking at failure more as feedback than defeat help you? And why?

_____

_____

_____

_____

In what ways could that freedom bless you? In what ways could it bless others?

ABOUT THE AUTHOR

Christopher Shiver is a certified N.L.P. Coach focused on 1-2-1 coaching for relationships and well versed in Ericksonian suggestion (hypnosis).

Born and raised on Seychelles islands, he has an eclectic background in Business Management, Entrepreneurship, Coaching, and Clinical Research. He holds an associate degree from New Mexico Military Institute and a Bachelor of Science in Psychology from Arizona State University, focusing on cognitive neuroscience. He is the co-host and coach of the Extraordinary Being Movement.

AUTHOR CONTACT INFORMATION

Christopher Shiver, *NLP Master Practitioner and Coach*
Website: ExtraordinaryBeingMovement.com
Email: chris@extraordinarybeingmovement.com
Social: @ExtraordinaryBeingMovement *(Facebook)*

CHAPTER 20

PARTERSHIPS CAN TAKE THE FORM OF MANY THINGS!

By Robert W. Jones

"Before you can work on your mindset,
you must work on your heart-set, and if there is alignment,
only then, will you pursue the appropriate skillsets
for success."

— Robert W. Jones

Partnerships can take the form of many things, from personal relationships to business arrangements to even team athletics. However, partnerships for the purpose of this discussion are 2 or more professionals owning and running an organization together. Partnerships can be beautiful because as they say, two minds are better than one. Partnerships are also beneficial because more capital can be sourced, division of labor can be assigned, separate expertise exists, and much more. But partnerships can also become ugly because disagreements of strategy, feelings of inequality, lack of equal passion and principle, life changes, and other descensions can arise.

In my 25 years of business ownership, I have had several partnerships that have started out with the best of intentions only to end in tragedy because of pride, a lack of communication, or just outright distrust. For years I had pointed the blame at my partners, from reasons such as they had lacked passion, they were not committed, they were difficult to work with. See a pattern here? it was always "they" in my thinking. In my original mindset, even though I "thought" differently, my actions were that "my partners were there to serve me." Not each other, which trickles over to the clients.

Can you see how that thinking like this created a setup for failure? Having the best mission, vision, strategy, and plan will never work if your partner feels that they are there to serve you, not the business, better yet, the prospects and clients. Believe me, I had my share of partners who treated me in the same manner, and it didn't end in a pretty outcome. Looking back, we probably picked each other. I was the first to see the hypocrisy in them, but at that time, I failed to see that the finger always led back to me.

Ironically enough it was not the "school of hard knocks" in business that taught me to think (and even feel) differently about "partnerships." It was an LCSW, who was also a certified life coach and entrepreneur. I had hired her because I had just come out of a failed marriage, failed business, a host of medical crises and I even had to sell my stake in one of my businesses to a "partner" to stay afloat. My life coach stated that many of my issues were not the partnerships. She stated that whether the goals, intentions, missions were clear and aligned, I would never move forward if I, myself, didn't trust!

The very reason I sought partnerships was that I wanted to be valued, relied on, heard, and trusted, but I didn't trust. I obsessed. I thought, "Are they doing their job? So, I micromanaged, I knit picked, I initiated the wrong conversations, and worst of all, I was attracting the very partners who were like me: partners who did not trust. They micromanaged, knit-picked, initiated the wrong conversations, and more. We attracted each other and, no piece of paper would keep us together, whether business, or life partnerships.

Although one day, things changed, my life coach helped me discover and accept one simple, yet impactful revelation, that trust was the underlying problem I had with partnerships. Partnerships in life, whether personal or business. I probably won't be able to help solve any trust issues that you may have, but from my experience, I hope to create some awareness. Through the coaching that I have received and some self-directed personal development I have found that there are some achievable actions that may help you move forward, as I have. These are principles that you can take to build trust and strengthen your partnerships. These 5 principles can help you immediately in your business partnerships (maybe even your personal partnerships).

The first principle I learned was to hold no grudges. A grudge is a persistent feeling of resentment towards someone. The problem is that anyone grudge may not be overly problematic, it is though, for those who give permission to grudges, they seemingly continue to stack them up until crisis. Resentment can manifest is in several ways, such as, it could be when you don't celebrate your partner's success, or that you work against your partner, or even that you secretly want them to fail. Now that is a disaster.

The second principle I learned was your turn, my turn. In business partnerships, success comes from partners having distinctly separate talents. It is true that the separate talents make for a broader and deeper level of serving clients, but what about taking credit for such service. I remember having a partner and it was always a struggle. We both stayed in our lanes, but when it came to taking credit, we both wanted to be seen as the symbol of that success. Our debate looked like this. Partner, "if it wasn't for my sale, we wouldn't have the client." Whereby I would say, "If it weren't for my designs, we would have any sales." By taking turns, or even sharing the credit, whether public or private, both partners can savor the spotlight.

The third principle I learned was when it comes to the big things, there needs to be two yeses. Or a majority. Big things can be different things to different partners, but it's important to understand when it comes to big things, create some boundaries or budgets to know. Set limitations, both in cost and time. For example, it could be a $500 level it could be $1000 level it could be $100,000 level. Or it could be let's allow 90 days for this campaign to work. However, when it comes to those big things, such as hiring a person, buying a new property, implementing a new marketing concept, your big thing needs to be 2 yeses, not a yes and a no, nor a no and a yes.

The 4th principle is to be never right, create options. I think in many ways this is probably the most important principle of all, when a person starts to be right all the time, they make YOU statements. These statements may sound like this, "You did this wrong" or "You couldn't get the job done" or "Why didn't you talk to me first." This "You-You" eco-system makes for a dysfunctional, negative environment for you and your partner(s) to move forward. Instead of attempting to be right, give options. Options may not feel optimal, at the end of the day, there is more synergy derived from the positiveness of conversation, not the negativity of being right.

The last principle I learned was to have compassion before criticism. This really is important because many times people look at criticism as a way to move forward, but criticism really is the operation of disapproval based upon perceived thoughts or mistakes and many times conversation and compassion will overrule that of criticism because truly if there are any opportunities to be found it's done through a compassionate the conversation that "seeks to understand, then to be understood" as Stephen Covey says.

All partnerships will go through their ups and downs. This list of principles is not inclusive of everything that can make partnerships better, nor is it meant to be. This list is to help create a starting point of awareness for you the business partner to achieve in a more effective and efficient way. As a Partner, Associate, Vendor, Client, Manager, even Spouse, etc., these principles can help you operate at a more optimal level. Think about it this way: These five principles will help get you to imagine better and faster. Facilitate and encourage, start with these principles and create a place where synergy can manifest and not disappoint.

Creating the right partnership is powerful, answer the following questions…

What's partnerships do you currently have in your life?

_____

_____

_____

_____

How do you view those partnerships? How do they serve you and do you serve them?

_____

_____

_____

_____

How do you manage the ups and downs of your partnerships?

_____

_____

_____

_____

About The Author

obert W. Jones is Founder and Chairperson of the iNETrepreneur Network, an omni-channel organization that offers Radio, Television, Learning Academy, Networking Events, and publishing, such as the iNETrepreneur Magazine, and the International Bestselling series, The Art of Connection. His organization has received an honor for a Networking Group of the Year, was a Launch Team member of Realtor.com, Marketing Director for E-Food Safety and Nuvilex, and is 2-time National Sales award winner with Chanel and Internationally bestseller Author himself. His company helps emerging entrepreneurs, business owners and influencers create awareness in affordable, high Impact ways.

AUTHOR CONTACT INFORMATION

Robert W. Jones, *Founder & Chairperson of iNETrepreneur Network*
Website: www.iNETrepreneurnetwork.com
Email: robert@networktogether.net
Social: linkedin.com/in/inetrepreneurnetwork

CHAPTER 21

WHAT DOES BEING A WARRIOR MEAN TO YOU?

By Frederick Martinez

*"We are warriors of the heart helping
each other rise above mediocrity."*

— Frederick Martinez

Being a warrior means being vulnerable, fearless, compassionate, trustworthy, resilient, strong, egoless, and powerful. It means being a battle-ready leader, confident you can and will take on anything that stands in the way of your mission. Because of your strong belief system, no obstacle or circumstance will stop you.

A warrior has a deep sense of faith, doesn't fear death, and is capable of sacrifice for the greater good. A warrior shows a way of being, a way of life that leads to overcoming challenges not through hopes but in faith. Because hope is a waste of time while faith is power. A warrior is the light in the darkness, the light that merges the mind, body, and soul.

A warrior is a balanced, impeccable leader because their thoughts and actions have direction and purpose. A warrior's balance comes from knowing the masculine and feminine energies. Regardless of your gender, the masculine energy takes action, and the feminine energy shows compassion, love, and care. Being a warrior means you know the values of time and energy in yourself and others. You aim tirelessly to increase love, compassion, and awareness within yourself and others by holding a high standard of integrity. A warrior sees and appreciates different perspectives in life. And through those perspectives the warrior gains knowledge and understanding.

A warrior lives the truth and fights for it. The truth exists in absolute vulnerability, removing the armor and revealing a person's soul. The truth is in the authentic self, knowing no individual person has all the answers. A warrior is not afraid to admit this.

A warrior's energy and actions are based on love. This foundation focuses the warrior on the good in the world, leading the warrior to fight for people who cannot fight for themselves. A warrior believes anything is possible. A warrior is willing to die to make this world a better place. A warrior doesn't live in fear or play victim to circumstances, limited beliefs, or conditioning from the past. Such living is powerless, but fighting those circumstances, beliefs, and conditioning will build strength and character.

Everyone may have their own definition of what a warrior means to them. Think about it, resonate with that. Visualize it, feel it, and use it to build the ultimate warrior inside you.

How Can You Benefit From Being A Warrior?

Using the traits of the warrior and embodying the warrior spirit, you will become unstoppable. You will have peace amid the chaos of life because you will be able to handle anything that is thrown at you.

You will adapt to the environment and circumstances around you, and you control your emotions. You will master resilience, or resilience will master you. You will embrace adversity and overcome any challenge. You will be driven to succeed no matter what obstacles are thrown in your path because you are committed to see it to the end.

You will know how to control your emotions. You will not give in to pain, knowing it is through the pain that you will grow. You will develop physical, emotional, and spiritual skills and these will strengthen you in your journey. You will learn that the heart is a sacred space where you build genuine connections with others.

You will begin to live in the present moment because life's pleasures are in the moment of feeling the other person's presence rather than in the memories of what could have been. You will begin to celebrate life because death is always around the corner and if you are not living your life then you are already dying.

You will begin to appreciate solitude because the path of the warrior can be a lonely one and one where few succeed. You will begin to relax and meditate daily to strengthen your mind–body, because otherwise you will live a stressful life. You will begin to live an extraordinary life, knowing you are safe and loved at every step along the way.

You will embrace the warrior's fight, which is for one reason alone: for love. The love of others, the love of life; love for what is good, for family, friends, and strangers. You will soon be in tune with your intuition, letting your internal spirit guide you in the right direction. You will embrace the mind–body–heart–soul connection and will always strive to learn more about your God-bestowed gifts. You will seek out clarity and understanding in every interaction.

You will always live and act with integrity. You will have a sense of priority for what is important over what is not.

You will have grit and strength to push beyond your limits. You will face life's fears and embrace failures; these failures will help you to succeed in life. You will have passion and appreciation for everything you do.

You will recognize that through discipline you get stuff done.

Finding Your Inner Warrior

Finding your inner warrior is about living your life on your own terms, using your experiences and circumstances as a guide to shape yourself into the warrior you want to be. Every warrior is different because of their circumstances. How will you overcome yours to honor the struggle and celebrate success?

A warrior rises out of pain, out of experience, out of the struggle. The warrior knows what it takes to complete their mission. Not everybody can be a warrior because it is about mindset rather than physical strength. You can push your body to extreme levels. What prevents you from making that push is your mindset. We quit in the mind before pushing the limits. To have a warrior mindset you have to train to be mentally tough. You have to put yourself into serious, difficult situations. Restrict yourself and have discipline. This mindset cannot be found by reading a book or taking a course. You need to start living your life and pushing yourself further and further every day, out of your comfort zone. You will fail in the attempts you make, and you will get back up to try again until you succeed. Through the experience of failure, getting hurt, you will become stronger and wiser. Your mind will become tougher and give you the drive, the fuel to achieve any objective. What happens after failure defines you.

The warrior in you shines out from your darkness, in the scorching fire that burns away your old circumstances, limited beliefs, negative thoughts. As you are renewed, the warrior in you rises from the ashes.

I did not always come from a place of love. I had to grow through a divorce to find the place of love, acceptance, forgiveness, and understanding. I learned to be the fertilizer that supports growth, and not the poison that stops it.

You have the choice to make this world a better place or a bitter place, to give so you leave this world a better place or to take away from it when you go. But when you invest in yourself, you join a tribe of elite warriors made by life's circumstances. You begin to enjoy the journey to finding your inner warrior.

Find your inner warrior, and answer the following questions...

What's your definition of a warrior?

_____

_____

_____

_____

How can you grow your inner warrior?

_____

_____

_____

_____

How will you begin building your tribe of warriors to change the world?

_____

_____

_____

_____

ABOUT THE AUTHOR

*F*red brings a wealth of experience and knowledge in the areas of optimal high-performance going from being the underdog to champion, teaching you to the way of the inner warrior mindset to eliminate your limited belief systems that are holding you back from achieving your success.

Fred has been an athlete for over 40 years, competing in all areas of sports ranging from baseball, basketball, football, tennis, powerlifting, and track. In college, he was a track sprinter at the division one level. After college, he had a dream to one day represent the United States in international competitions. The journey to become an Olympic weightlifter started after watching it on Olympics. His dream came true, representing the U.S. at world cup competitions and the Pan American.

Despite never being the tallest, biggest, fastest, strongest, or smartest athlete and student, he approached every day like it was an opportunity as a gift from God and to do whatever it takes to improve and learn from his mistakes. Fred motivates and inspires others, planting the seeds of greatness to embrace the underdog that's inside you as fuel to become a champion in all areas of life.

He is certified in *Neuro-Linguistic Programming* high-performance coaching, certified in sports performance hypnosis, USA Weightlifting Sports Performance Coach, six sigma green belt certified, has a degree in electrical engineering and is the author of the "Financial Game Plan For Your Dollars and Cents: A step by step common sense approach to making the right financial decisions.

Fred is one of the co-founders and co-host of the Extraordinary Being Movement.

AUTHOR CONTACT INFORMATION

Frederick Martinez, *High Performance Coach*
Website: ExtraordinaryBeingMovement.com
Email: fred@extraordinarybeingmovement.com
Social: @ExtraordinaryBeingMovement *(Facebook)*

CHAPTER 22

YOUR STYLE CREATES YOUR LIFE, THERE'S JUST NO WAY AROUND IT

By Stan Cole

"Feel amazing, look amazing, BE amazing"

— Stan Cole

*I*sn't it odd that we are defined in this world by; the way we look, the house we live in, the car we drive, the friends we have, the job we do or any other such external factors? How is it that style & image became primary aspects of our identity? We are, and will always be, judged by the way we look first and foremost. This is a fact that will not change anytime soon.

It's interesting to think that even though others place judgment on us based on our image, and even though our future is inextricably intertwined with those placing judgment, fashion education is still nonexistent. Society has found it unnecessary to teach the importance of style, clothing, image and their impact on our lives. We are never truly taught how to look or what to wear, beyond dressing appropriately for a job or interview. We certainly were never taught how what we wear impacts what we can create in life. Up until now our process of dressing has been based on our parent's position in life: Emotion, opinion, and activity. Creation & intention have never been primary to our dressing process.

But here we are in the future, understanding that we are the creators of our lives. Today we know that our image means everything. We know that what we wear tells our story, or a story, without us ever speaking a word. People look at us and quickly determine the kind of person we are, how much money we make, who our friends are, the kind of home we live in, what we do in our free time and more. It's time for us to create our story rather than being defined by it. It's time to get intentional with the creation of our future and direct our attention to our style & fashion.

I want you to play a game - a game of transformation. I'm asking that you try something new. I understand that new things can be scary, but I assure you the results are extraordinary when you push through your fears and gain the wisdom acquired by traveling through the unknown.

In this game you will create a new persona(s). Not once, not twice, but every single day. Imagine a story with sensational characters. A Character(s) that has everything you want in life: Money, work, relationships, traits, mindset, and anything else you can think of. Every day, become one of these characters. Dress like them, take action like them, be responsible like them, make decisions like them, and react to adversity like them. As time goes by modify your character(s), enhance them with new & beneficial qualities. Combine imagination with reality and watch the results unfold. Watch your life transform as if by magic.

Stop thinking about the person you are. Give all your attention to these characters you create. Characters that have everything you want. Get to know them. Begin to dress how they dress so you can feel how they feel and act how they act. There is a reason we have an admonition to walk a mile in someone else's shoes. When you put yourself, literally, in their shoes, you will feel as they feel and gain new understandings.

How you dress will alter how you perceive and are perceived. As you shift your style, and interact with people, they will immediately notice your new look, followed by your new attitude. If you enhance your style (playing into this game of life and adapting to the norms of society), those you interact with will be uplifted and their feedback will add to your strength and ability to assimilate your characters' traits. Over time these characters will fade and a brand new you will be left in their place. This is a cycle, and it never ends. We are human. We will always want more in life so that we can be more and create more. This is a blessing. We are here to expand not stagnate. Learn to love this game of transformation. It has the power to magnify all that you can become and create.

Difficulties may arise in this game because we have not been taught to look within ourselves for a variety of personas. I promise you; your mind will resist. This is normal. It is because you're moving out of your comfort zone and your mind wants to keep you safely where you are. Also, you have not exercised this muscle. Just as you would hire a trainer to achieve quicker results at the gym, there is a professional that specializes in bringing you faster results in your transformation. This person is called a transformational stylist. Take a leap of faith, take action, and hire one. They will help you excel in this game and win time after time. Invest in yourself so that you can more quickly level up in life. Do what you've never done before and I guarantee you, the results will be astounding.

For a moment, imagine that you are a rock uncut and raw. Before you are chiseled you have no brilliance or shine or color. You are shapeless and awkward, hardened and burdened by years of pressure and exposure to the elements. Suddenly one day a transformational stylist sees your potential. They see you for what you can be rather than who you are. Their gift is to imagine & create something yet unseen. They begin to chip away at your external facade until they see the sunlight shine through. Inspired by their imagination and progress, they continue to chisel away, uncovering your internal beauty bit by bit with all their tools and insights. The change is uncomfortable, even unbearable at times, but your desire to see the results overshadow your discomfort. After weeks, maybe months, of crafting and polishing they hold you to the light and are blinded by your brilliance. Your hidden facets, revealed by their efforts, reflect the light in a way not seen before. You have been transformed from a rock into a diamond that sparkles bright and powerful.

Your image is the visual expression of your thoughts. Play my game. Begin creating new characters that have everything you want in life. Imagine multiple versions of you. Be intentional with these characters, leave no detail to chance. Every day, in every way, live as they would live through the ups and downs of your life. Do this, and you will find yourself living a life you have only dreamt of.

Your style is a catalyst for creation. We know the only constant in the universe is change. You will change with or without your intention. Be Intentional, alter your image and you will improve all areas of your life. Through style you will discover a new world, and a transformational stylist will show you the way.

Having your own personal style tells a lot...

What's your personal style?

_____

_____

_____

_____

If you had no limitations, how would you change your persona? And why?

_____

_____

_____

_____

How will you feel being in this new role? What opportunities would it provide you?

_____

_____

_____

_____

About The Author

Stacyann goes by Stan for short. She is an Arizona native, two-time state gymnastic champion and Olympic hopeful. Her gymnastic career, coupled with her college education, yoga teaching, and other significant events, provided the foundation necessary to succeed and excel in entrepreneurship and in life.

Stan is a survivor of two suicide attempts. She deeply understands the darkness that can befall us as well as what it takes to survive and eventually thrive in life.

Her entrepreneurial life began in the fourth grade when she started selling packs of gum for profit at school. Her love of fashion was also born at this age. During her limited spare time, she was devoted to scouring her sister's fashion magazines, tearing out the pages and creating dream boards of her future.

Today she is the successful owner of a mindset coaching and style transformation business that helps individuals grow beyond what they thought possible and at the same time she guides and/or amplifies their ability to create massive success and fulfillment in their lives. Her purpose is to inspire awareness, hope, faith, fun, curiosity, and possibility.

She is the mother of two fabulous adult children and two rescue dogs and a cat. In her spare time, you can find her with her animals or, of course, shopping.

AUTHOR CONTACT INFORMATION

Stan Cole, *Style Transformation & Mindset Coach*
Website: getstyled.club
Email: Stan@stancolesinc.com
Facebook: @getstyledbystan
Instagram: instagram.com/_.getstyled
LinkedIn: linkedin.com/in/stancoles
TikTok: @msstancoles

PILLAR 3

ACTION

CHAPTER 23

LIGHTS, CAMERA, ACTION!

*"Take action! An inch of movement will bring you closer to
your goals than a mile of intention."*

— *Steve Maraboli*
Life-changing Speaker, Bestselling Author,
and Behavioral Scientist

What a fantastic journey we have been on so far! I know the stories, strategies, and tips these amazing coaches have provided will assist you on your journey. We have learned about the importance of self-awareness and the power of growth, and now we will explore pillar three, ***Action!***

Have you ever found yourself wondering at the end of the day what you accomplished? I know I have. Many of us tend to look at "busy work" as taking action in life but being in action is much more than that!

Taking action is about being intentional and doing the "right things" that will lead us to where we want to be and produce the result we are looking for. You need to ask yourself, *"What are the best actions to achieve the result I'm after?"* It's easy to be busy and "doing things," but are you intentionally doing the "right things?"

Every day we make a lot of decisions based on amazing ideas, like deciding to start a business or get healthier or continue our education. Unfortunately, these decisions and ideas don't mean much if we don't put effort into turning them into actions we can actually take.

Action is a muscle that you need to develop! Most people never move from deciding to doing because they haven't built the habit necessary to be in action. We are held back by insecurity, fear, and excuses. We see the overall goal as being distant and hard to get to, when really the path is a series of smaller steps that are easy to accomplish. You just need to take that first one!

When you don't allow yourself to take that first step and be in action, you are doing a disservice not only to you, but to your family, your friends, your community, and your business. Who knows if your next idea could change your life and those all around you?

All the time I hear people say, "Someday I will do that" or "When I find time later." The next thing you know later becomes years, and the brilliant idea you had has now been done by someone else. Yikes! Who wants to see that? I challenge you to **commit** and take action! You don't need to wait for everything in your life to be perfect before you make that next step. Getting bogged down by ego and worrying about how others view us keeps us from making dreams a reality. Just start taking small steps and practice being in action.

To make your ideas a reality, take the time to create a plan, rely on clear and achievable goal-setting strategies, and build the habits necessary to create ongoing success. Sometimes, it takes just doing *1% More* to create that next million-dollar idea.

Let's be in action and take a few minutes and answer the following questions...

What idea have I thought of and still not taken action on?

_____

_____

_____

_____

What do I feel that is holding me back?

_____

_____

_____

_____

What small actionable steps can I take today to begin being in action?

_____

_____

_____

_____

What impact would committing to action have on my life?

_____

_____

_____

_____

CHAPTER 24

CREATING A SYSTEM THAT WORKS!

"Each system is perfectly designed to give you exactly what you are getting today."

— *W. Edwards Deming*
- American engineer and management consultant

To be effective in achieving goals, you need to design a system appropriate to your lifestyle. Without an effective system in place, you will have a hard time seeing what is working and what is not. Having a system gives you the power to stay organized, focused, and on track to achieve more; it is effective because it helps you to conserve self-control for when it's needed most.

So, what is a system?

A system is something you do consistently, a routine that increases your odds of achieving happiness. It is built on the daily habits and strategies that you assemble together to provide you the energy and momentum to cause acceleration and growth.

The best way to think of systems is with this acronym that I created …

***S.Y.S.T.E.M.*™** - *Strategies You String Together Energizing Momentum.*

There are a number of great personal and business strategies that you can adopt to take steps toward your goals, but without creating an easy-to-use system specific to your lifestyle, those strategies may not work effectively. Many strategies fail because people lack a clear vision, an adequate plan, or proper implementation. Sometimes people are simply too afraid of change or failure to start and act consistently.

In this chapter, we are going to explore how to create a system by using effective strategies that will create that *1% More* difference in your life. You will be able to develop a clear vision and a simple plan for implementing your strategies with confidence!

What you first need to decide is what you want to achieve. This may be an easy question for some of you, while others of you may find yourselves more challenged at coming up with an answer. Think about it and try to visualize what you may see ahead for this year. Take a look at your life right now, and then think about where you want to be and where you want to go. Start by brainstorming and writing your ideas out on paper or on your tablet. Allow your mind to move freely among the ideas you have stored inside.

Having a vision helps you with your journey, provides you with a sense of direction, and ultimately takes you to your destination. Many people avoid fully fleshing out a vision because they believe they'll never really be able to achieve it. They are content to just pass the time away, living an ordinary life. They have no vision, no long-term goals, and no idea of how to do more than get by day-to-day. In comparison, those who are successful have created a vision to guide them. Having such a vision will likewise allow you to change your life, and each change offers an additional opportunity to clarify your vision.

Quite simply, a vision is your *"Why"* and forms the bigger picture. Your vision defines and describes who you want to be, what you want to be known for, what you want to accomplish, and what difference you can make in the world. Your vision provides a framework to understand and assess your long-term goals, which are the smaller, individual experiences that build up to your accomplishments.

Your vision should be answering questions like *Why is this accomplishment important? How will this make a difference in my life? Who else does it impact and why? How would it affect them? What more do I want out of life? What do I want less of in my life? What new skills do I want to learn? What do I need to feel whole and complete? When I'm gone, what would I want people to say or remember about me?*

To create a vision, you must first identify what matters to you. It will guide you in designing the system that is essential to taking action toward growth and impact. Creating an actual vision statement is an opportunity to go deep and explore the question of what matters to you. Your statement doesn't have to be perfect, but it lays the groundwork for further exploration. It will also assist you in tough times to bring you back to your whys, realign your life for balance, and of course, get you back on track.

Start by listing your skills, knowledge, resources, and abilities. Then come up with a list of categories you want to explore, such as health, relationships, finances, family, and new experiences. Create your vision statement by combining what you can or want to do with the skills you already have, with the areas that need improvement.

Here is an example of my vision statement…

"I transform people's lives through the power of coaching. This desire drives me to serve others and guide them in finding internal peace and happiness. Coaching is essential because a single positive change in one person's life can have massive ripple effects in the lives of many, and I want to be part of that process for as many people as possible."

With this vision statement, I can build a foundation to develop my plan of action. I like to develop a plan that can be completed every six weeks. A six-week cycle gives me the opportunity to make changes and adjustments as needed. It's a short enough time period that I can stay focused, work consistently toward my goals, and still build new habits needed to manage my time more effectively. At the end of six weeks, I can reflect on what I have completed, and relax and reward myself for working hard.

I recommend the use of a six-week cycle to my clients, and now to you. I also have tips for how to structure your action plan:

1. Decide what you want to achieve for the first six weeks. Give yourself a theme! This allows you to make it fun and keeps you focused on what you wish to accomplish.

2. Begin each day with a healthy positive routine which could include working out, walking, mediation, reading, or daily affirmations. Start your day with intention, so you can stay focused on goal-creating activities and problem-solving tasks.

3. Create a daily time management schedule for the next six weeks and block out 30 to 60 minutes a day for personal development, health, finances, self-care, date night, family time, and other important well-being activities.

4. Design your six-week action plan. For the first four weeks focus on being in action, actively pursuing the goals you have set and doing the correct activities to get you there. Don't fall into the trap of thinking that "busy work" is getting you closer to your dream. Be intentional and centered on goal-achieving activities. Your fifth week should be about feedback and review. Check for any problems that have arisen and review ways to resolve them, so you don't fall off track. This week is a great space to recognize your blind spots and uncover

new opportunities for growth. Evaluate what is working and what is not. In addition, you start planning your next six-week cycle, creating new themes and strategies while reviewing the current ones. The sixth week is for self-care and celebration. You have worked hard, so make sure you reward yourself!

Remember, there is no one perfect system. The system has to be the right fit for you, your lifestyle or business, at this particular time and must evolve as you evolve.

Let's put your system into action, and answer the following questions...

What is your big "Why"? What is motivating you to create action?

_____

_____

_____

_____

What is your vision statement? Write it out below ...

_____

_____

_____

_____

Start planning out your six-week cycle. What will the theme be? What actions will you take for the first four weeks? How will you celebrate and reward yourself?

_____

_____

_____

_____

CHAPTER 25

LEVELING UP YOUR GOALS!

*"You are never too old to set another goal
or to dream a new dream."*

— *C.S. Lewis*

All great ideas start with a dream, an abstract concept that we want to bring to life. Your dreams could be anything–starting a business, finding love, speaking on stage, or becoming an author.

Even if your dream is not well defined yet, know that anything can be achieved when you take proper, actionable steps.

Creating a system that will help you make your dream a reality involves creating and establishing goals that enable you to produce tangible results toward real progress. Goals grow out of your vision statement; without a clear vision, intention, and a practicable plan, your dream will likely fizzle out before you even get started.

Did you know? Many of us adopt New Year's resolutions, only to let those resolutions burn out days or weeks later. According to a study by Discover Happy Habits, of the 41% of Americans who make New Year's resolutions, only 9% feel they are successful in keeping them to the end of the year!

Achieving our New Year's resolutions and goals can be challenging. Many of us create unrealistic goals, underestimate the time needed to reach them, and fail to keep track of our progress. All of this causes discouragement, stress, and a sense of failure. To set realistic goals, it's important to understand what exactly a goal is.

The best way to explain it is with an acronym I created: **G.O.A.L. = Great Outcome At Last!™**

A **Great Outcome At Last!™** represents a more significant purpose that you wish to achieve. Sometimes our goals are driven by ego or by external forces, like our culture or someone else's wants and needs. But really your goals should be about what YOU want to achieve. They need to align with your true aspirations and bring you happiness, meaning, and joy.

Goals need to be clear and specific and have measurable outcomes to help you stay focused. Learning how to set goals effectively helps you take your dream to a new dimension. One of the best tools to set appropriate goals is the **S.M.A.R.T. Goal** framework.

S.M.A.R.T. Goal helps you clarify your ideas, create a plan, be clear, and focus your efforts by using your time and energy wisely. The acronym stands for **Specific, Measurable, Achievable, Relevant, and Time-Based**.

Let's take a look at what these words mean and how you turn a goal into a **S.M.A.R.T. Goal**.

S = Specific - Your goal should be clear and specific. What exactly do you want to achieve?

> **Example:** *I want to get more fit by exercising 5 days a week at the local gym.*

M = Measurable - You need to track your progress. What evidence can you present to show you are making progress?

> *Example: I will create a daily exercise plan, record how many days I go to the gym, and keep track of my weight on a weekly basis.*

A = Achievable - Is your goal achievable? Is it realistic and attainable within a reasonable time frame?

> *Example: I will exercise for an hour a day, 5 days a week, to lose 5 pounds by the end of the month.*

R = Relevant - Is this goal in line with your values and long-term objectives?

> *Example: I will cut out drinking alcohol and eating unhealthy foods, so I will have more energy and can begin to lose unnecessary weight.*

T = Time-Based - What is your time frame to achieve your goal?

> *Example: I will evaluate my progress every 30 days to see what is working and what is not, in order to make adjustments.*

Using the *S.M.A.R.T. Goal* framework is an effective tool that provides the clarity, focus, and motivation you need to achieve results. It is easy to understand and to use. It allows you to discover any hiccups and revise as you go along. Keeping this framework in mind improves your ability to reach your goals by encouraging you to define your objectives and set a completion date.

Incorporating goal-setting into your system for action is critical to keeping you focused and moving forward. But no matter how well you plan and define your goals, you will find that challenges arise along the way. That's why I also like to view my goals as problems that I can solve. Think of goal-setting as dealing with your basic wants and needs, while problem-solving adds value to your outcome.

A ***problem-solving*** approach expands your thinking to find more opportunities and better resources to achieve your goal. Problem-solving allows you to brainstorm further questions and take a different approach to find additional solutions to achieve your goal. While goal-setting techniques focus on achieving a result in the long term, problem-solving looks at how steps toward your goal may be resolved in the short term.

Let me explain it like this using the fitness example above: on day 15 of your 30-day plan, the gym has to close for a few days to make building repairs. You don't want to give up the progress you've made or skip working out, so you think of other ways to get your exercise for those few days. You decide to jog in the park with a friend and discover that you love being out in the fresh air. Not only have you found a solution for the problem of not being able to go to the gym, but you've discovered an activity you enjoy and can add to the rotation.

Problem-solving creates space to explore your goals by looking at new opportunities. It's a place to strategize options and gives you the ability to find valuable solutions to achieve more in less time, with fewer failures. Adding a problem-solving approach to your goal-setting allows you...

- flexibility and freedom to make adjustments along the way. You can choose to take specific actions that might be more beneficial. You are in control of what you can reach today.

- to create systems that effectively help you make better and faster results. It also allows you to become more resourceful. It allows you to take actions that are simpler and repeatable.

- to be more committed to the task at hand and more willing to see it through. Your goals have more meaning and are aligned with your passions and mission in life. You will feel more motivated because you are focused on your long-term purpose.

- to build leadership skills. Making more decisions as you evaluate what to do next, why it's essential, and how to do it hones your ability to keep moving forward. You learn to be more detail-oriented and can track your results, not just measure them.

As you can see, combining the two approaches is very powerful! *S.M.A.R.T. Goals* assist you in figuring out your wants and needs. The process gives you the ability to set specific, measurable, and time-based goals to reach your dreams. *Problem-solving* fills in the "gaps" to identify issues, their causes, and new solutions to help you take the next step. It provides you the perspective to understand where you are and where you want to be and helps you to stay motivated and focus on achieving your goals.

Setting goals are powerful, answer the questions below to get started...

What goals would you like to achieve in the next 12 months?

_____

_____

_____

_____

Pick one goal and turn it into a S.M.A.R.T. Goal (Specific, Measurable, Achievable, Relevant, and Time-Based).

_____

_____

_____

_____

What obstacles might you face in achieving your goal?

_____

_____

_____

_____

How would achieving this goal make a difference in your life?

_____

_____

_____

_____

CHAPTER 26

BREAKING BAD, CREATING NEW HABITS THAT LAST!

"Habits change into character."

— Ovid, Roman poet

Goal setting is an important part of creating a system to take the action needed to get you closer to making real changes in your life. Another important aspect of creating an effective system is understanding how old habits are holding you back and how you can create new habits to move you forward. So what exactly is a habit?

A habit is a thing we do every day, an action that becomes a ritual or an automatic and subconscious behavior. Some habits are good, like brushing our teeth, tying our shoes, or exercising. Habits can be cultivated or eliminated; they can also form without us even intending to form them.

There are three types of habits - ***Unconscious Habits***, ***Deliberate Habits,*** and ***Damaging Habits.***

- *Unconscious Habits* are things we do without realizing it because they are ingrained in us, and we haven't stopped to think about them. These habits can be positive or negative. Examples include biting your nails, making gestures when you speak, going out of your way to please people, or engaging in negative self-talk.

- *Deliberate Habits* are habits that propel us forward toward our goals and priorities. These are actions we choose to make part of our lifestyle. Examples are exercising regularly, eating healthfully, making a budget, or reading daily. These are habits that have a clear purpose and focus.

- *Damaging Habits* are those that serve us at the moment, but not in the long term. These habits may alter our moods and reduce stress, but some of the patterns can turn into an addiction, with short-term benefits and long-term costs. We usually know they are wrong, but we continue to do them anyway. Examples are binge eating, smoking, being with people who don't appreciate you, wasting time on the internet, and so on.

Good habits are essential to our health and well-being in life. Studies show that about 40 percent of our daily activities are performed not based on active decisions but on habits. Having habits allows us to free up energy to focus on other tasks and to be more creative. They provide us with routines that help us work more efficiently.

Habits become the routines that define who we are, good or bad, and they are there for a reason. They provide some benefit, even if overall they are bad for us. Some of the benefits are emotional, like staying in a toxic relationship knowing it's terrible for you. Other benefits are biological, like drinking, smoking, and drugs. Many of these more significant damaging habits extend into smaller bad habits. Luckily, all habits can be changed and improved upon for higher success and a more fruitful life.

The most effective way to change a habit is to replace it with a new one. The creation of a new habit, when repeated, triggers the brain to develop a new neurological pathway and grow new neurons. Developing new pathways encourages goal-directed action, and helps a person be able to adapt to change. Unfortunately, the old pathways are not actually deleted; they are always there, and it's easy for the brain to fall back into old habits.

Understanding what psychologists refer to as the *"Habit Loop"* can explain the importance of developing new habits.

In the book, The Power of Habit, Charles Duhigg describes the "Habit Loop" as consisting of three main parts; ***Cue, Routine,*** and ***Reward.***

The Cue is a trigger from the environment that tells your brain to go on autopilot. This is an automatic mode or routine (mental or physical) that gets turned on when the cue is present. For example, every time you go to a movie theater and smell hot, buttery popcorn, you start to feel hungry. Cues can also develop from repeated motions, like sitting down at your desk at work or plopping down on the couch in front of the television. These cues have a pattern and may be triggered by a location, the time of day, a particular person, an emotional state, or a movement. The more the cue is repeated, the less we pay attention to it or how we react to it.

The Response is the behavior you automatically perform after the cue has occurred. Routines can be physical, mental, or emotional. For example, you pick up your phone and scroll through social media when you feel bored or bite your nails as a response to stress.

The Reward is what you gain from the habit. The reward closes the loop and reinforces the routine. There are beneficial rewards, like feeling good after eating a healthy meal. There are also less beneficial rewards that can reinforce habits you don't want to keep, like spending an entire weekend binge-watching television. Your brain will begin to wire that behavior to the reward. Even when you don't realize it, you will crave that behavior.

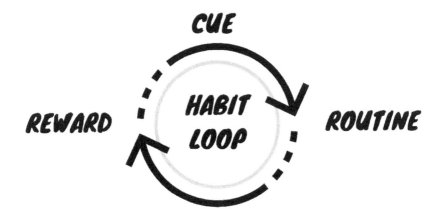

We build destructive or bad habits because of the built-in reward system. Drinking, drugs, and smoking are easy habits to adopt because they spark your brain with the neurotransmitter dopamine. They naturally reward your brain with a pleasurable sensation even though they damage your health and well-being.

On the other hand, positive behaviors like exercise, eating healthy, and meditation doesn't necessarily have immediate rewards. It takes repetition to build the habit that will eventually stimulate the brain in a positive way.

Breaking bad habits requires you to become self-aware and to practice new behaviors. Change is possible with all things, as long as you have the desire to change.

The first step to breaking a habit is to ***identify the routine***. Ask yourself, *what do you want to stop doing?* Is it drinking alcohol? Always being late? Drinking too much caffeine?

Once you identify the habit you want to break, you can begin to eliminate the undesirable behavior by ***creating a new reward***. Rewards are very powerful, and I recommend experimenting with this process to find what will satisfy your craving. You need to ask yourself, "What am I really craving from this routine?" Do you drink and party too hard on the weekends in order to avoid responsibilities? To get attention? To trigger dopamine release?

There may be more than one reason you've built a habit and experimenting with different rewards can help you discover what exactly your brain is looking for. Using the example above, maybe you can start with hanging out with friends in a alcohol-free environment. If you find that despite engaging in social activities, you still feel the urge to drink, sociability may not be the reward your brain craves. The next thing may be to try positive activities that trigger the release of dopamine and replace a craving for alcohol.

This is just one example, and the reasons people develop habits can be complex, so experimenting with the reward may be necessary to break and replace old habits with more fulfilling behaviors.

Once you have identified the routine you want to break and have found a more suitable reward, the next step is to create what is called an ***implementation intention***. Create a plan for what to do when a particular situation arises. The process needs to include the who, what, when, where, and how specifics that are necessary to produce successful results. This uses the If-Then structure: ***"If situation X occurs, then I will do Y."*** For example, "If I feel hungry between lunch and dinner, then I will snack on an apple instead of chips."

Much like adding a problem-solving approach to working toward your goals, creating a specific plan to deal with possible issues gives you a greater chance of making the new habit stick.

Understanding what habits are and how to change them makes it possible for you to achieve significant results. This process requires self-discipline, determination, and patience. Learn to become mindful and observe your behaviors to explore the issues behind your habits so you can control them and not allow them to control you.

Take a moment and review your habits, and answer the following questions…

What bad habits do you have that are affecting your life?

_____

_____

_____

_____

Think about one bad habit and identify the cue that is setting it off. (Think about the location, time of day, other people, emotional state, or an immediately preceding action.)

_____

_____

_____

_____

How would eliminating this one habit make a 1% More difference in your life?

_____

_____

_____

_____

What is the routine that follows when this habit is triggered?

_____

_____

_____

_____

What reward results from continuing this habit?

_____

_____

_____

_____

What new behavior would produce the reward you desire?

_____

_____

_____

_____

What implementation intentions can you use to stop yourself from going back to the bad habit? ("If situation Y occurs, then I will do X behavior.")

_____

_____

_____

_____

Let's continue being in action! Our quest continues with stories and strategies to learn how to create change, build happiness, learn the power of self-care, and how to be in control of your mind and body.

CHAPTER 27

CREATE AND LIVE FREE

By Jeremy Nicolaides

"Have the courage to follow your heart and intuition. They somehow already know what you truly want to become. Everything else is secondary."

— Steve Jobs

There I was, walking through the wonderful wizardry world of Harry Potter, and it wasn't a theme park. I was in an old airplane factory outside of London. The company I worked for had flown me first-class from Los Angeles for a 45-minute meeting with the Director and Producers. As Global Creative Director for a company specializing in 3D movies, I was at the culmination point of an eight-year journey.

Back in 2002, when I got a job with a visual effects company working on Sesame Street 4D for Universal Studios, Osaka, I had no idea about the world of 3D movie making. I can still remember my first-time wearing 3D glasses. The movie screen disappeared, and I was transported to an exciting, immersive world. I was hooked!

In the following years, I would jump at every opportunity to take on more significant roles. 3D movies became my passion. I was winning awards and accomplishing things that had never been done before. It was awesome!

Between the success of James Cameron's Avatar and other widely successful 3D movies, my value in Hollywood skyrocketed. Calls were coming in from all over the globe for me to consult and run 3D projects. An exciting time!

From one consulting job, I became the Global Creative Director for a post-production company building a global army of artists for all the new 3D films in Hollywood. We went from 50 people in Hollywood to a team of 3,500 worldwide. I remember having nine major Hollywood films going at once. It was exhausting!

My goal with this story is not to impress you. It's to show you how I went the traditional route of climbing the professional ladder and how I had what most would consider a dream job. The reality is, after the dust settled from our global expansion, I felt a lack of fulfillment. What was I doing? Long hours, no weekends, and poor health, for movies that would come and go in a week or two. Plus, I was making someone else wealthy.

Why accept working for fifty years with no guarantee of a life of freedom at the end?

Eventually, I was offered a position in Vancouver, BC, because the LA office was closing. However, I still couldn't shake the feeling that I was in a soul-sucking job. I walked away!

Over the next year, I was able to decompress. What did I wish to do with my time? Diving deeper into landscape photography, I decided to be a professional photographer, but how would I replace the salary I had left behind?

After doing some research, I purchased a print and marketing company to support my photography business. Plus, produce passive income.

Wow! I had no idea what I didn't know!

I came in with so much confidence after being a pivotal player in building a global company serving the world's top filmmakers and movie studios. Surely, I could turn around a mom-and-pop business!

The short story is that trial and error nearly bankrupted us. By the way, we were newlyweds (a fairytale love story for another time!). Every problem was costly. It was brutal!

I remember coming home from work one day and finding my wife in tears. "What's wrong, babe?" I asked. "I have no idea how we're going to pay our bills at the first of the month!" She was scared, and her concern was justified. By this point, we had spent our savings, maxed out all of our credit cards, borrowed money from the bank, and had already asked the family for help.

Long gone were days of disposable income. Now it was peanut butter and jelly sandwiches with water. Things were bad! I thought entrepreneurship and owning a business would set us free! Instead, for the first fifteen minutes of each day, I wished I had a job so I could call in sick or quit. We were in the most challenging situation of our lives. All we could do was keep going.

While listening to entrepreneurial and business podcasts, I learned about coaching programs and masterminds. What do I have to lose? I signed up. This decision would become our big turning point.

I took this new information and restructured the business so that eighty percent of it was passive. With the extra time, I was able to create several other streams of income. I was back on top!

A great comeback story, right? I land this cool, extraordinary job paying me a ton of money, realized there was no fulfillment for me, so like a high diver in the Olympics, I dove into what turned out to be a scary dark valley of despair. From there, I clawed my way back to the top after learning from the coaching program and modeling success.

Here's the catch: I wasn't living free. I was still trading my time and health for money in this cyclical path of burnout and pullback, never taking care of myself. Sure, I was making good money, and on the surface, it all seemed great. But I was unhealthy, not eating correctly or taking care of my body, and enduring an enormous amount of stress. It was all wrong.

Of course, my relationships suffered too. "Where did you go?" my wife would often ask. I didn't go anywhere. She could tell that I was somewhere else mentally, either thinking about business or so exhausted, I zoned out.

Did you know that in the mid-70s, the term "burnout" began to describe people who were overworking themselves because they exhibited the same symptoms as drug addicts? Think about that! We give up precious time (limited), trade health and relationships for money (unlimited), and experience physical and mental symptoms similar to drug addicts. Crazy!

Something had to change.

Something has to change!

It's archaic to think that working 9-5 for fifty years to get ten years of freedom, hopefully, is a good plan. Additionally, why do we strive to attain personal fulfillment and gratification from work when it isolates us from our family, friends, and community?

No more! It doesn't have to be this way!

The world has changed; we can be successful, happy, and free.

Thinking deeply, I realized I needed a significant mind shift away from the status quo and I wasn't alone. So, how do we create our desired lifestyle and generate success?

> *"Those who make more money than you don't work ten times more hours than you, and they're not working ten times harder than you. They know something that works ten times better than something you know." —Myron Golden*

At Golden Octopillar, our motto is *Create And Live Free*. We help creative entrepreneurs and business owners create lives of freedom and success. Gone are the days of climbing corporate ladders and burning ourselves out. Now, we work less and make more. We are *Lifestyle Creators*, and we *Create And Live Free!*

Would you like to unshackle yourself from a life that doesn't serve you and get on the path to personal and financial freedom? I want to share with you the foundational strategies and principles I discovered on this journey.

Get free access here: www.GoldenOctopillar.com/Freedom

Let's create and live free! Answer the following questions…

Are you trading your time and health for money? In what ways?

_____

_____

_____

_____

How does this trade make you feel?

_____

_____

_____

_____

Describe what freedom would look like for you if this was no longer necessary?

_____

_____

_____

_____

ABOUT THE AUTHOR

Jeremy Nicolaides is a multi-award-winning film industry veteran known for successfully collaborating with filmmakers, producers, and studios on such films as Dune, Godzilla vs. Kong, Avengers: Endgame, and Blade Runner 2049.

Throughout his career, Jeremy established himself as a key creative and knowledgeable business executive, from Chief Creative Officer and Global Creative Director to Executive Producer. Jeremy applied his knowledge and business development skills beyond Hollywood to successfully execute the purchase, turn-around, and sale of a print and marketing business and built a successful consulting company.

Today, Jeremy runs Golden Octopillar: A business helping creative entrepreneurs and business owners work less and make more while living a life of freedom. Believing in a new breed of human, one that can be happy, successful, and free, Jeremy will guide you away from a life of burnout and self-sacrifice to a fun and full life where your money and business work for you. Now, through Golden Octopillar, he encourages creative entrepreneurs and business owners to challenge the status quo by defining their own reality and creating opportunities to design their lifestyles. Jeremy Nicolaides is a Lifestyle Creator who Creates And Lives Free.

AUTHOR CONTACT INFORMATION

Jeremy Nicolaides, *Lifestyle Creator*
Website: www.GoldenOctopillar.com
Email: Jeremy@goldenoctopillar.com
Social: https://linktr.ee/GoldenOctopillar
Free Training: www.GoldenOctopillar.com/Freedom

CHAPTER 28

PLEASE PLACE THE MASK OVER YOUR OWN MOUTH AND NOSE BEFORE ASSISTING OTHERS

By Alexis Braunfeld

"Let food be thy medicine and medicine by thy food"

— Hippocrates

How do we care for others if we don't care for ourselves? I love being an entrepreneur. I love helping other entrepreneurs. Most of us are hardworking, many-hat-wearing, one-person shows. However, in order to take care of others, we need to take care of ourselves. Too often, we do not do this. For too long, I had that problem. Then I learned how to be part of the solution.

Beginnings

I have always been an entrepreneur. I grew up on a small farm in Pennsylvania. I was surrounded by nature. There were horses, plenty of outdoor activities and a bountiful summer garden. My mom made jelly and bread from scratch and worked all summer putting home-grown vegetables on the table. She also instilled in me a love for crafting. My mom is a veterinarian, and my dad is a real estate investor. They both influenced me with their entrepreneurial endeavors.

As a child, I sold painted seashells and string bracelets. In middle school, I baked cupcakes and cookies and sold them to my classmates. By high school, I had discovered jewelry design and metalsmithing. I loved the craft and design aspects of the work. I received my BFA in Metalsmithing and a Gemology degree. I thought this would be a path to my own business. But it wasn't. I worked in the jewelry world and honed my skills. I worked in wholesale, retail, and still work a little in the business. But I realized that, although I loved crafting it, jewelry never was my passion.

Cake Creations

It wasn't until after I became a mom that I realized my passion for Sugar Art. I started constructing elaborate cakes for my children's birthday celebrations. Eventually, people started asking me to make similar creations for their special occasions. After filling cake orders for a few years, I began teaching a course on cake decorating at a local craft store. I dove right in. I juggled a lot. I was a mom by day, a cake artist by night, and taught classes too. I wanted it all. And I wasn't taking care of myself.

The teaching job was meant to be. All along my journey, I had tried to do everything myself but didn't have the skills to do it all. When a prospective student called up to request a specific class time, I was able to offer her a class that worked with her schedule and, as it happened, no other students signed up for that particular class. As it was just the two of us, Gina and I chatted a lot during the practice time. We soon found out that we had very similar entrepreneurial spirits and dreams.

After about two months, Gina called me and asked if I would consider starting a business together. I had my reservations because I already had a few clients, but I said yes. It was the best thing I could have done. She was organized, a trait that I lacked. I could think outside the box where she could not. We meshed well and, in February 2013, we started Sugar Treasures. Sometimes you just don't know the missing piece until you stumble into it.

Burn Out

I stopped teaching and we dove into our business, slowly building it up. We were both stay at home moms. We would put our kids on the school bus and run to our shop to bake and sugar sculpt. It was amazing and fulfilling …and exhausting.

Back To The Farm

Around this time, I was invited to a wellness event by a friend who was focusing on wellness education - promoting nutrition and healthy lifestyles. These health professionals said that we need nine to thirteen servings of fruits and vegetables every day to manage our health. My family didn't eat anywhere near that amount. I ate salads and my kids had their obligatory three bites at every meal. My eyes opened to the connection between nutrition and health. I started to think about my children's health.

My son had struggled with chronic health issues, including constipation and asthma, from a very young age. He was taking a daily adult dose of MiraLAX at the age of two-and-a-half years old and on a daily inhaler by the time he was four. It seemed as if he was always sick with some kind of virus or infection. My daughter was mostly healthy, but she also had recurring cases of strep throat and suffered from high fevers. I thought this all was normal. All little kids get sick. Right? The final straw was when they each had simultaneous cases of strep throat that lasted a month. I was pulling my hair out trying to care for my children while running a business.

I decided to change how we ate. I started researching which ingredients were good and which were not. I learned to buy better products than the ones I had been purchasing. Gone were the products loaded with added sugar, color dyes, too many preservatives and other ingredients that I couldn't even pronounce. I made changes to our pantry, started adding more whole food to meals, and began growing our own vegetables. We started to flood our bodies with fruits and vegetables.

Over time these changes really made a difference. My kids were healthier. When they did get sick, the illnesses were less severe and did not last as long. My son was able to stop taking MiraLAX and now we only keep his albuterol inhaler just in case of an emergency. I had always had a minor issue with bleeding gums, and I noticed that my gums had not bled in months. This real-life experience showing the connection between nutrition and health was mind-blowing. Equally important was the fact that I suddenly had the energy. I had been lacking at work.

Simple Solutions

I was now on track running the cake business and caring for my family but now, as the always curious entrepreneur, I wanted to help others learn how to be healthy. I looked at my own life. I loved my cake business but did not love the stress that it caused. I still wasn't taking care of myself. I put my family and business before my own needs. That needed to change. In addition to the dietary changes, I started making sleep a priority, I began drinking more water and added daily walks to my routine. I slowed down the cake business and added wellness education for families and entrepreneurs. Now I get to do it all! I am helping guide families and entrepreneurs to better nutrition with simple solutions. It is amazing teaching people how to get onto a trajectory of health that will stay with them for life. You can do, and be, anything you want. But when you're reaching for the stars, don't forget about self-care!

Let's start taking care of ourselves by answering the following questions…

What are the signs that you are heading towards burnout?

_____

_____

_____

_____

What ways are you providing self-care to yourself?

_____

_____

_____

_____

What type of healthy routine can you put in place to reduce stress?

_____

_____

_____

_____

About The Author

Alexis Braunfeld is a mother, sugar artist, and wellness educator. Through counseling, group support, and classes, she works with individuals, groups, and families to provide simple health solutions. These solutions lay a foundation of health for life.

Alexis learned the importance of self-care while attempting to meet the various competing demands that entrepreneurial parents face. Mom by day and cake decorator by night, she believed that she could do it all but, like so many, struggled finding balance. Exhausted by the press of life, Alexis realized that, if she was not taking care of herself, then she could not take care of her children and clients. With this epiphany, Alexis discovered a new passion.

Inspired by the positive results of implementing easy nutritional changes and a daily exercise routine in her own life, Alexis began helping others.

Many entrepreneurs ignore their health while focusing on their business. This is where Alexis comes in: providing solutions that fit easily into busy lives and improving those lives with one simple change at a time.

AUTHOR CONTACT INFORMATION

Alexis Braunfeld, *Expert in Balancing Wellness & Sugar Creations*
Website: https://linktr.ee/alexisbraunfeld
Email: alexisbraunfeld@gmail.com
Phone: 610-608-3030

CHAPTER 29

CHOOSING HAPPINESS

By Carrie Vee (Verrocchio)

*"People are just about as happy
as they make up their minds to be."*

— *Abraham Lincoln*

Ha.

Ha Ha.

Ha Ha Ha.

Ha Ha Ha Ha.

Ha Ha Ha Ha Ha.

Ha Ha Ha Ha Ha Ha.

Ha Ha Ha Ha Ha Ha Ha.

Ha Ha Ha Ha Ha Ha Ha Ha..

I know you just skimmed over all of those ha-ha's. You know you did. You looked at the cascading ha-ha's and decided that you could read one ha-ha and know what it said, and you would just move on to the meat of the chapter and ignore all of the ha-ha's.

Don't get me wrong - I don't blame you. You read the chapter title, Choosing Happiness, and you were already feeling a bit befuddled and maybe even a little angry. CHOOSING happiness? When did happiness become a choice? Happiness is dependent upon circumstances, isn't that what you've been taught? You wait for situations to be happy in order to laugh. You don't laugh just because. Right?

I am going to go against the grain and what we have been taught in our past throughout this chapter. Having happiness and joy and fun are indeed a choice. Therefore, I want you to go back to the opening ha-ha's and I want you to read each one of them out loud. Every single ha-ha. Go ahead, I'll wait.

For most of you, you got to about the fourth line of ha-ha's and you started to laugh. Sincerely laugh. Because reading ha-ha's out loud is silly. And silly makes you laugh. And the truth is - you can pull out silliness, laughter, and joy in the most dire of circumstances.

When my mother recently died, we found things to laugh about. We miss her deeply. We are grieving deeply. Yet still, we found something to laugh about each day - at least one thing. Mom loved our dog, Gisselle, and we would laugh about how Mom would toss her dog food, one piece at a time, on the floor and Gissells would chase after the food. They loved their game and we found laughter in recounting that memory.

When my grandmother and brother died, my dad made sure that he brought laughter into our lives even as we grieved. When my dad died, we remembered that lesson and brought in laughter and joy even as our hearts were breaking.

It's an important lesson to learn and remember. You can choose happiness and joy or not. And the choice is entirely up to you.

The Bible says that when the Apostle Paul was in prison, he was singing. Despite his circumstances, he chose joy and happiness.

How many times have you found yourself in a situation that is miserable and feels like it will never end? I'm guessing that is how the Apostle Paul felt in that prison. And if Paul could choose happiness, so can we.

Choosing to be miserable leads to energy blocks and being emotionally stuck. What if we chose to reframe the situation, as we talked about earlier in this book? The fact is that many times if we are going to be happy and joyful it is because we are going to have to make a conscious effort to choose it. Plain and simple. Life isn't always going to go our way. That's okay. Things not going our way is no excuse to choose to be miserable.

We can choose to smile, or we can choose to frown. Both take energy so why not choose the positive energy? We can create a pathway to happiness in our brains if we want to.

When I am doing a photoshoot, the photographer will often say, "Okay - big laugh!" The cool thing is - even if I happen to be having a bad day, once I begin to fake laugh, a real laugh follows. I immediately feel lighter in spirit, more positive, and ready to choose happiness and joy despite what may be going on in my life. That's why I gave you all of the ha-ha's at the beginning of this chapter.

I love the quote by Abraham Lincoln: "People are just about as happy as they make up their minds to be." The first time I read that quote, I was admittedly a bit angry. Make up my mind to be happy? What about all of the losses in my life? What about all of the pain and sadness? What about all of the times things didn't work out the way I thought they would? I am supposed to make up my mind to be happy despite all of that?! The answer for me - and for you - is YES.

The truth is - no-one gets through life without emotional scars. So why are some people happy and joyful and others not so much? Because we have a choice, and that choice determines how we will live our lives.

May I suggest that we embrace more fun in our lives? May I suggest that we deserve fun and joy? May I insist that we laugh more and celebrate joy? I am absolutely sure that you just gave me a resounding "YES" - followed by an equally resounding "HOW?"

Okay, let's be real. We are BUSY people. We have jobs. We have housework. Add in families, appointments, daily commutes and commitments and caring for everyone around us - who has time for FUN?

And at the time of the writing of this book - did I somehow forget that we have been going through a pandemic? We are forced to meet virtually. We are tired of Zoom. We just want to hug our friends again. We want to network, get out, live the way we used to - without masks, without fear, without suspicion. We are split between the vaccinated and not vaccinated and both sides have their reasons and opinions... and more tension and division builds.

Despite all of that, am I really going to hold onto my opinion that happiness and joy come down to choice? Am I seriously suggesting that we find time to add PLAYTIME into our lives? Are we in kindergarten?? Do we really need recess?

Listen - before you tune me out - playtime, fun and joy are NOT something that should be a low priority. Yet, we often overlook them. We view playtime, fun and joy as unnecessary - they are more privileges afforded to few. They are something to feel guilty about. In the hustle and bustle of life, the things that make us happy are drowned out by all the clutter, noise, and daily demands and drama that close in on us.

But it isn't just about fun and games. It's about our mental, physical and emotional health. And it's crucial.

Don't believe me? Keep reading.

George Bernard Shaw is quoted as saying, "We don't stop playing because we grow old; we GROW OLD BECAUSE WE STOP PLAYING."

Read that as many times as you need to. We don't stop playing because we grow old; we grow old because we stop playing. I don't know about you, but I want to be a fun grandma. I want to be that woman that everyone says, "she's HOW old? She acts so much younger than that!" I want to be that person that everyone thinks is so fun that they can't wait to hang out with her and laugh together. It's way better than being known as the grumpy one, don't you think?

I believe that most of us WANT to have more fun. It just isn't as easy as it used to be. In grade school, we had recess. We were sent outside for FORCED playtime. In fact, we went outside every day and played. If it was cold, we bundled up. If it was raining, we played in the gymnasium. In the summers, we rode our bikes, went swimming, and soaked up the sunshine. And we didn't feel guilty. Not one little bit of guilt. We loved having fun, we looked forward to having fun, and we had no problem making time for fun, happiness, and joy in our lives.

Now, we feel guilty when we have fun - mostly because others aren't having any fun, because we perceive having fun as a sign of laziness or lack of motivation to get our work done, or because we just don't feel worthy of fun. We state lack of time as an excuse for not having fun. We convince ourselves that fun is for children and when we get older it's time to be serious. We are grown-ups now. It's time to embrace grown-up things. I'm all for maturing. But when did maturing become synonymous with not having fun, not laughing, not being happy, and having no joy?

How many of us have heard and lived by these statements - "Work before pleasure." "First work, then play." I get it. But taking a "recess" is a smart thing to do, and science is giving us the nod and smile that we need to prioritize fun, happiness and joy and make them a part of our daily lives. Even when we're busy. Even when we are in the midst of a project. Even during a pandemic. Even when we are tired of virtual meetings. Even when others call us lazy and irresponsible for having fun.

How many of you have had something like this in your lives:

The day is gorgeous. The sun is shining, there is a gentle breeze. There is a smell of flowers in the air. The essence of fresh cut grass is tempting you to come outside- take a walk, wiggle your toes in the warm grass, smell the honeysuckle, and pick some fresh blueberries and tomatoes. BUT. You keep working. Ignoring the call to take a much-needed break and have some fun. You will just finish one more hour. And then you will take a quick break to laugh and enjoy that sunshine on your face. A walk with your dog. A call to a friend or family member. But that hour goes by. And then another. And another. And then you finally decide to go outside. But the clouds have moved in, the rain has started, or it's time to cook dinner. The window of opportunity has closed. And you realized that you had not been working efficiently anyhow because you REALLY NEEDED THAT FUN BREAK. You knew you could have created a pocket of happiness and joy amidst your workdays. But you chose not to do so.

Disappointment moves in. Regret takes hold. Sadness overtakes you.

Let's look at the science:

What does fun even mean? According to the Oxford Dictionary, fun is "amusement, especially lovely or playful." And even though WHAT is fun is defined by each person individually - and what is fun for me might not be fun for you - having fun IS crucial.

Science suggests (and I agree!) a few reasons to have more fun.

Reason Number One: Incorporating more play time, more fun, happiness and joy into your life improves your relationships at work and in your personal life.

Having fun with others helps to build trust and develop communication. We connect in ways that simply working cannot accomplish. When we laugh together, we connect with each other. It strengthens bonds. Studies show that couples who know how to laugh together are happier. Friends who know how to laugh together, who choose happiness and joy, develop closer friendships. When companies incorporate time to just have FUN, productivity increases. Job satisfaction increases. Customers are happier. Retention rates are higher.

Have you ever had the privilege of working in a company where fun, happiness and joy were prioritized? I have. And I have also worked in companies where fun, happiness, and joy were frowned upon. In the former, the employees worked better, the customers were happy, and the company was flourishing. In the latter, the complete opposite was true. Lack of happiness, lack of joy, lack of fun created an atmosphere of mistrust, dissatisfaction, and high turnover rates. All of that trickled down to the customers, who were highly dissatisfied. Not a good way to run a company in my opinion.

Reason Number Two: As if reason number one wasn't a good enough reason to have more fun, happiness, and joy, how about the fact that having fun makes us smarter? AND more profitable.

It is far more fun to be more profitable than less, wouldn't you agree???

If you ask me, that's a darn good reason to embrace fun, happiness and joy. And since I have the stage right now, I get to give you my opinion. Having more fun, embracing happiness and joy, makes us smarter. That is pretty cool stuff right there.

Science tells us that having more fun, laughing in happiness and joy, improves our memory and concentration. So going back to my sunny day example, taking the fun break results in greater concentration and focus when we return to work. I can live with that!. If we follow that logic through, it's actually lazy to NOT take the break, right?

Studies show us that reading for fun improves our language skills and math proficiency. Studies also show that reading for fun can protect us from that cognitive decline that often comes with age. So pick up that novel and get smarter - and ward off dementia. I will tell you, my mother was an avid reader right up to the end of her life. From the time I was a little girl, I can remember my mother having a book in her hands. She fell asleep reading a book - sometimes the book would still be laying over her face when she woke up (see, I'm giving you a mental image to laugh at right there!). In the years she lived with us, I would check on her every night before I went to bed. You guessed it, she was either reading a book...or had fallen asleep reading a book. She was a smart woman - lesson learned.

Additionally, fun, happy, joyful activities introduce us to new ideas and concepts that lead to better self-directed learning. Just having fun introduces us to new ideas. And if that wasn't enough proof for you to have fun and embrace happiness and joy, read on.

Reason Number Three: Having fun helps to reduce stress.

We don't even need science to prove this one. Having fun, choosing happiness and joy, is a powerful antidote to the stress that we carry around in our lives. Studies show that laughter reduces negative emotions and helps to decrease negative feelings - even in a stressful situation.

That saying, "laughter is the best medicine" is true. That isn't to say we don't ever need medicine. I'm not suggesting that at all. I am suggesting that we add laughter, fun, happiness and joy to our daily lives to help alleviate pain and stress.

As I mentioned in the chapter on grief, when we experienced death in our family, we laughed as well as cried. We cried over our losses - which were devastating. But we also laughed at the fun memories. That laughter helped ease the pain and deal with the loss. Laughter, happiness, and fun helped us to move through the grieving process.

I recently watched a documentary entitled "Heal" - which I highly recommend, by the way. One woman shared about her cancer journey. When she was diagnosed with cancer, she decided that she was going to laugh - a lot - every day. And she did. She and her husband watched funny movies and laughed. Not surprisingly, her cancer tumors shrank. It was such an interesting concept that with my own cancer and Lynch Syndrome diagnosis at the end of 2020, I decided to increase my laughter, happiness, and joy - for the rest of my life. If cancer was going to try and take me down, I was going to go down feeling joy and happiness. But interestingly enough, I recovered quickly from my surgery and cancer recovery. I am convinced that laughter brought quicker healing.

When my mother was diagnosed with stage 4 aggressive terminal cancer in May of 2021, she took it in stride. She didn't lose her sense of humor and she didn't stop laughing. She was smiling when she died and gave my husband a strong "good morning!" on the day she died. Laughter, fun, happiness and joy make a huge, positive difference in our lives.

Add laughter to your life. I mean, unless you are enjoying all that debilitating stress.

Reason Number Four: How about this one? Science shows that having fun in physical activities balances your hormone levels.

I don't know about you, but I am all over this one! Science has shown that high stress levels negatively influence our hormones (think cortisol!). Stress also negatively affects our endocrine, metabolic, and immune functions.

But by consistently choosing happiness and joy and fun recreational physical activities, we can balance our hormone levels. Riding a bike. Taking a walk. Dancing. Going out in a canoe. Skiing. Find what is fun for YOU and incorporate that fun into your life.

I spent decades living under extreme stress. I completely annihilated my hormones. All of the hair on my arms and legs fell out. My eyebrows and eyelashes fell out. My hairline receded. I was a complete physical mess. I may never again have hair on my arms and legs. My hairline may never be the same. Thankfully my eyelashes have come back in, but my eyebrows are sparse at best. I am working with a naturopath now to balance those hormones that I destroyed by never making time for fun, happiness and joy and instead living in a fight or flight mode for so long. My naturopath's number one recommendation? Have fun. Laugh more. Stop taking life so seriously. Choose happiness and joy.

How's that for a recommendation? Let go of the stress and fill that time with laughter, happiness and joy. It isn't going to happen on its own, people. We have to CHOOSE it. Think about what is fun for you and make time for it.

Reason Number Five: This is a good one. Fun can make you more youthful and increase your energy.

WHAT? For REAL?? Think about it for a moment. Stress is draining. It sucks the life right out of us. It makes us tired, cranky, miserable, and no fun to be around. We must get rid of those characteristics. Who wants life sucked out of them? Not me! And not you, either, or you would have stopped reading this chapter by now - or ripped it out of the book calling me "Crazy CarrieVee."

By reducing stress and instead having fun, choosing happiness and joy, we boost our vitality. Why do we leave all of that energy and vitality to children? Are they the only ones who "deserve" recess? I think not.

Plato professed that life must be lived as play. And let's go back to George Bernard Shaw, "We don't stop playing because we grow old; we GROW OLD BECAUSE WE STOP PLAYING." We Grow old because we stop playing.

Let's start playing more. Embracing more fun. Decide today to CHOOSE happiness and joy. At the end of this chapter, I am going to give you some fun ideas that you may want to incorporate into your life. Feel free to add to this list.

For now, let's dive into HOW to choose to have more happiness and joy in our lives. It really is easier than you think.

Start with Counting your blessings. Happy people choose to focus on the more positive aspects of their lives. They set their minds on a specific reason to be grateful. And here's the thing. The more they focus on the positive, the more they realize how much they have to be grateful for. There is always something for which to be grateful. That attitude of gratitude brings happiness and joy into your life.

Next, as we discussed earlier, smile! Force yourself to smile if you have to, but smile. Your facial expression, as we proved earlier in this chapter, can influence your brain. You can actually program yourself to experience happiness by choosing to smile. In addition, you will start to encourage the people around you to smile. It's a win-win situation. You will increase your happiness level while at the same time help others to increase their happiness levels. So get smiling.

Another way to choose happiness, fun and joy, is to stop yourself from verbalizing a complaint. The next time you want to verbally lash out against someone, a situation, or even yourself don't. Just don't. Instead choose to be humble and keep it to yourself. You will defuse an unhealthy, unhappy environment. Even better, you will experience joy and happiness by choosing peace over being right. I have heard it said you can be right, or you can be happy. It's your choice. Choose happiness.

Choosing happiness and joy is easier when you speak daily declarations into your life. Keep speaking daily declarations into your soul. A declaration is a positive thought, an affirmative belief. It is a personal statement of truth. Used daily, declarations can reduce stress, build confidence, and improve the way you see life.

As a side note, If you are interested in receiving daily declarations and journal prompts sent directly to your cell phone (only in the US for now), send me a message at carriev@coachcarriev.com and we will get you added to the list. My clients and friends find these declarations and journal prompts a powerful tool in choosing happiness, fun, and joy in their lives.

Waking up with a morning routine in mind is another way to choose happiness, fun and joy in your life. Just because you may need an alarm clock to wake up, it doesn't mean you have no control over your morning routine. I encourage you to wake up a bit earlier and establish a morning routine that will lead you into Radical Empowerment. Start your day the way you want it to start. Perhaps add in some stretching, drinking water, listening to a podcast, or doing some personal development reading or listening. Perhaps you will choose to have devotions and journal your gratitude. Whatever your morning routine is, make it yours. I encourage you to not check email or social media first thing in the morning. That practice gives someone else control over your day. Take back your control. I promise you the rest of the day will be so much better!

Yet another item on the pathway to choosing happiness is to choose one important task that you will accomplish each day. Happy people know there are demands on their days. They also know they have dreams and goals, and they know they want to contribute to the world. They operate out of the satisfaction of knowing they will accomplish at least one important task each day. They write it down and they get it done. When they go to bed, they sleep well knowing they have accomplished the one task that moves them forward. And that elicits happiness and joy in their lives.

Treating each other with respect will also increase your happiness and joy. Deep down, we want to give others the same respect that we would like to be given. We want to be treated with kindness. Do unto others as you would have them do unto you is a golden standard to cling to. This benefits both the giver and the receiver. It ends up bringing happiness and joy into the lives of everyone involved.

Focusing on your strengths will naturally increase your happiness and joy. We have strengths, we have talents. When we are walking in those gifts, we feel accomplished. We feel alive in the fact that we are living a life of purpose. Walking in those strengths helps us find our happiness and joy. Choose to use your gifts every day. Find an outlet and shine.

Finding some time to meditate and be alone is another way to choose happiness and joy. Our world is noisy, and it is imperative to take time to withdraw from time to time and sit silently. Technology can be overwhelming and can leave you drained and grumpy. Let meditation fill your cup and bring you happiness and joy.

Another way to choose happiness and joy is to look for benefits in your trials. Nobody gets through life without any difficulties. When you go through a tough time, find the joy hidden in the trial. Remind yourself that this too shall pass. Search for and find the meeting behind the trial. If nothing else, you are building perseverance by going through the trial. Additionally, you are learning how to comfort someone else when they go through a similar circumstance. Someone once told me that when you are going through a trial, take great notes. Someday you will help someone else on a similar journey. And that brings happiness and joy as you help someone else in need.

Last but not least, choose a healthy diet. I'm not talking about weight reduction, calorie restriction, or macro counting. I'm simply saying to choose healthy foods most of the time. Food has been known to affect our moods. To avoid an emotional crash, do your best to avoid overly sugary foods much of the time. Too much sugar can cause major fluctuations in your blood sugar and can cause wild mood swings. Also avoid skipping meals. You are not too busy to eat even if at times you try to convince yourself that you are. Eat when you're hungry. It will help to stabilize your mood and thus your ability to choose happiness, joy and fun.

Choosing happiness and joy, choosing to incorporate more fun into your life, is easier than you think it will be. Read through the suggestions above and think about how you can incorporate them into your life. You are worth choosing happiness. You are worth choosing joy. You are worthy of recess and having fun.

I tend to attract clients that want to be happy. They just don't always understand how to be happy because they believe their environment will never be aligned with what they want. The thing is, it doesn't have to be aligned all the time. Happiness, joy, and fun are a choice. Are you willing to choose them? Or will you spend the rest of your life waiting for happiness to happen to you? I hope you will choose the former.

I promised you a list of ways to have fun. I would love to hear what you add to this list:

- Play with your dog. Or cat.
- Laugh with your friends. Your kids, Your family.

- Dance with your significant other.

- Finger-paint.

- Play with a Nerf football.

- Grab your hula hoop and swing those hips.

- Pick up the pompoms and belt out a cheer.

- Keep the mistletoe up all year. Why not?

- Play with the frisbee that you tucked away years ago. Or buy one.

- Go axe throwing. I never knew how fun it was until I tried it!

- Spin in your office chair. Right now. Do it. Spin. GO

- Learn a joke and tell a joke. You go first. Knock, knock? You knocked.

- Bust a move the way that YOU bust a move.

- Do a puzzle. Hide a piece of the puzzle so you will be assured of being the one to finish it. My dad always did that, and we STILL laugh about it years after he's been gone.

- Call an old friend.

- Write a letter.

- Eat breakfast for dinner.

- Embrace the fun. Laugh. Live. It's your choice.

"Don't wait to be happy when things get better. Choose to be happy and joyful now - despite your circumstances."

— *CarrieVee*

Choosing Happiness Writing Exercises:

Start your own list of ways you like to have fun. Then circle those things you are actually incorporating into your life.

_____

_____

_____

_____

Go back to the list again. This time circle one thing that you will incorporate into your life this week.

_____

_____

_____

_____

Go back to that list again and decide that you will incorporate every item on your list into your life.

_____

_____

_____

_____

Keep adding to your list. You are worth it!

About The Author

Motivational Speaker, Published Author, Podcaster, and Certified Transformation, Forgiveness, and REBT Coach, helps those who have forgotten how to dream, overcome their excuses and live the life they were created to live.

She is the founder of the Radical Empowerment Method, an online program designed to walk people through the exact method she herself used to move from a life of feeling invisible to a life of empowered success and action.

Her newest book, *The Radical Empowerment Method: Getting Off the Sidelines of Your Life and Stepping Into Your PowPow Shoes*, is now available on Amazon. CarrieVee believes that choosing gratitude is foundational to a radically empowered life. Her first book, 30 Days to Gratitude Journal, available on Amazon, explains how the daily practice of written gratitude can and will transform your life.

After going from burned out corporate general manager to seizing opportunities and creating the life had been dreaming of, CarrieVee uses her experience to motivate and lead others on a journey of Radical Empowerment.

She is a Toastmasters Semi-Finalist in the 2020 World Championship of Speaking as well as a keynote speaker for Toastmasters. In addition, she competed in the Summit of Slay Speaking Competition and was chosen as one of the top four speakers. CarrieVee has been published in the second edition of "88 Ways Music Can Change Your Life," available on Amazon. She has spoken on numerous stages to thousands of men and women motivating and empowering them to live the life they were created to live.

AUTHOR CONTACT INFORMATION

Carrie Vee (Verrocchio), *Founder of the Radical Empowerment Method*
Website: www.coachcarriev.com
Social: https://www.linkedin.com/in/carrieverrocchio/

CHAPTER 30

WHAT ARE MY FIVE LOVE HIGHLIGHTS?

By Nicole Harvick

"We can send, receive, and feel love even through miles or through separation. Love can permeate your soul regardless of time or space. The power of love is unmatched by anything tangible."

— Nicole Harvick

Following my profound experience on the Big Island of Hawaii in 2014, I realized that I was in need of deep healing. That healing came through forgiveness, which continues to be an essential element of my journey, revealing the significance of loving ourselves.

The concept of love, the feeling of love, and my inner knowing, even at my age, has shown me that there are so many things of which I am capable. I wish to share with you my appreciation for what I am learning and encourage you to discover for yourself what is possible.

1. What is Love?

This question is asked by many with a different answer from each individual. For some, it's an intense feeling that resonates within their soul. For others, it is a feeling of uncertainty and uneasiness. However, I think almost everyone would agree that love is the most powerful of all emotions.

One of the reasons that love is so challenging to describe is because it can be used in many forms. You can love your pet. You can love a lifestyle. Sometimes, we throw love around rather carelessly, although I feel the most powerful and intense love for my children. It is a reliable and unconditional love I will always experience.

The word love also expresses the human emotion of kindness, affection, and compassion. When these emotions are felt, it is said to be one of the purest forms of love.

2. Are We Taught to Love?

I believe that when we arrive here as newborns, we are gifted from God our ability to love. Love is what our journey here is all about, as described by a verse in the Bible with which I deeply resonate.

"So, God created mankind in His own image, in the image of God He created them; male and female He created them." Genesis 1:27

I believe that when God gazed upon us as His creation, and we gazed back at Him, it was through eyes of love.

As we continue on our journey here on this earth, the beliefs of our parents, teachers and peers in school, and teachings of religious communities can condition us. I believe we learn to judge, bully, and criticize other humans. We can become egoic, self-absorbed, and critical. Each of these mutually harmful conditions I refer to can be changed when you practice loving-kindness and, most of all, acceptance of others who we perceive as different from us. If it's true that we are made in God's image, we are very powerful. What could be better than to walk through this life with love as our compass?

3. Stages of Love in a Relationship

Attraction
A glance, a double-take, a sly smile, and eye contact; there is always something that gets your attention. And then what? Maybe a quick conversation to see if you have anything in common. And if that answer is yes, the first date. The anticipation and nerves combined into one. And then relief, you like each other and agree to meet again.

Romance
It's going quite well. Candle-lit dinners and walks in the moonlight when there never seems to be enough time to finish the conversation and feeling butterflies every time you see their phone number pop up. You're both full of anticipation. Ah, bliss!

First argument
It was bound to happen; an argument. Now what? All of a sudden, they have flaws that you had never noticed before. Now, you question the relationship. You begin to see some differences of opinion. Then an epiphany; they are not perfect after all. What now?

Reality
You have both fallen off from your respective pedestals. And this is when the relationship begins—two individuals with unique ideas and motivations. Then the questions arise. How do we maneuver this curve? When you finally acknowledge that your partner has dreams and frustrations—just like you—the work begins.

Partnership
When you have seen their weakness and faults and allowed them to see yours, you also share appreciation for each other's strengths and

resilience. Now you can lock arms! You find your commonality. With mutual respect and love growing you realize that coming together as a couple makes you an unstoppable team. While it will never be perfect, the experience is worth it.

4. How to Love Yourself and Others

We can explain love in many ways.

For me, love is a deep feeling in my heart that I extend to others unconditionally, expecting nothing in return. Love is in the present moment. Love is knowing I can count on someone when I need them, and they can count on me in return. Out of love, I keep my word or a promise that I make.

Loving myself first is the key. Being kind and patient with my flaws, taking care of myself mentally and physically, allows me to love others. Loving myself reminds me of my worth.

Love is about respecting me and the other person, knowing when to agree to disagree and when to stay humble. Love is about living in gratitude and giving thanks for all my blessings. The ultimate gift is knowing how to both give and receive love.

5. Love is the Highest Vibration

Love is an energy and emotion we all wish to experience. We desire this feeling to move within our hearts and resonate within our souls. While love is intangible, we feel the presence. We can't force love. Have you experienced meeting someone who ignites the love already inside you? Do you feel how you can include them in that love, like magic? True and lasting love blesses us with the deepest of heart connections.

When I returned from Hawaii, I began to notice the word Ho'oponopono, everywhere; in a magazine, in a bookstore, in a conversation. When I listen closely, which I do, I intuitively knew it meant something and there was more for me to learn. Ho'oponopono is an ancient Hawaiian forgiveness practice that consists of four short sentences: I love you. I'm sorry. Please forgive me. Thank you. I learned that forgiveness is the stepping stone to abundance, clarity, kindness, and compassion—transmuting inner darkness into light.

Being humans, we know there is no such thing as perfection. With love, there is also suffering, with tears of joy and tears of sorrow. Going through my divorce—drawn out over years—was debilitating to my soul. There were moments of anger and wonder. For every situation, there is a yin and yang. Even though love is beyond definition, by being open to give love and receive love, we experience perfect gifts. Let's approach everything with an open heart and watch the world around us shift with awareness of miracles. Love is a feeling unmatched by anything in this universe. We can learn to surrender each day to feel this incredible power we call love. May the blessing of love find you and permeate your life with joy and wonder.

Let's create and build upon love in our lives, and answer the following questions…

What does love mean to you?

How do you love yourself? How do you show love to the people in your life?

What ways can you increase your vibration for love?

_____

_____

_____

_____

About The Author

*N*icole Harvick is an author, speaker, and passionate advocate of forgiveness. Her books include *Boy on a Swing* (2018), *"The Gift of Forgiveness"* in the book, *Unstoppable* (2019), and *"The Alchemy of Forgiveness"* in the book, *The Lemonade Stand 2* (2021).

Nicole is the CFO (Chief Financial Officer) of "Don't "Diss" Abilities," a 501 (C) (3) Tax-Deductible Non-Profit Organization in Arizona.

She is also the designer and creator of "The Ho'oponopono Bracelet" ® in addition to candles and oils. Nicole is certified in healing methods including Certified Ho'oponopono Practitioner, Certified Ho'oponopono & EFT Practitioner, Reiki Master, Certified Level 1 Tuning Fork Therapy, Certified in The Quantum Course of Energy Healing, and Certified Level 2 Mastery of Energy Healing. In both Arizona and South Carolina, Nicole enjoys kayaking, reading, yoga, hiking, and an almost-vegan diet. She is the proud mother of two adult children.

AUTHOR CONTACT INFORMATION

Nicole Harvick, *Passionate Advocate for Forgiveness*
LinkedIn - https://www.linkedin.com/in/nicole-harvick-4409a5a/
Facebook - https://www.facebook.com/nicole.harvick.90
Social: @Nicole Harvick *(Clubhouse)*
IG @nicoleharvick@Nicole S Harvick (Instagram)

CHAPTER 31

REVEAL YOUR ROCKSTAR!

By Darryn Yates

"Anyone out there who has a voice deep down telling you that you are capable and deserve so much more...that voice is right."

— Darryn Yates

I played by the rules. I did everything I was supposed to. I followed my dreams. I was a good guy. I come from a good hard-working family. I pursued something I loved.

So, what happened? I was near-broke, depressed, hopeless, and hiding in my car. My wife Crystal thought I was going to a job that just fired me. I was experiencing excruciating lower back pain from a bulging disc. I needed surgery but just lost the insurance. My wife was pregnant with kid #3 and we needed help with the upcoming baby bills.

I had two choices: I could stay on the dark path I felt myself on OR I could figure this out, make my family proud, and be truly happy.

223

My name is Darryn Yates. I am from Granite City, Illinois, near St. Louis Missouri. My parents are both well-respected retired school teachers. My mother, Carolyn, worked in Special Education and became an administrator. My father, Ron, was a football coach who taught physical education and health. My younger brother, Damon, works with troubled youth.

I grew up an athlete, but the music bug bit me in 10th grade. I had knee surgery that kept me out of sports for a bit. During this time, I was asked to sing in a local garage band. It seemed right as my room was wallpapered in my favorite 80s rock bands.

I rebelled against authority; being the son of school teachers wasn't easy for me. Any little thing I did wrong, my parents would hear about it. Being a rock singer was something I could call my own. Plus, my mother loves Elvis Presley, so maybe that had something to do with it.

I made a deal with my parents after graduating high school. They had heard me talk about CA for two years now. If I went to one year of college nearby and still wanted to move to CA, they would help me get out there if I got my college degree.

After one year at Illinois State, I was in tears and pleaded with my parents to help me get to CA. I not only wanted this, I needed it.

I enrolled in San Diego Mesa College. I also started dabbling in modeling, acting, and music.

After 18 months, I transferred to Cal Poly Pomona, an hour east of Los Angeles. I finished my bachelor's degree two years later. I majored in Radio & TV Production. It was now finally time to move to LA. This was the city I knew I had to be in to fully experience the music & entertainment business.

I lived in Studio City, Marina del Rey, and Venice Beach. After a few years playing in bands and working at record labels & music management companies, I started my own all-original rock band, On Tracy Lane. OTL opened for several national acts, did music videos including one with actress Lacey Chabert (Mean Girls, Party of 5, Hallmark Channel), toured the country, flew overseas to play for the US troops, and had a couple small record deals.

I then moved to Nashville TN where I started a music publishing company and licensed over 15 of my songs to film, TV, and commercials.

After a couple years in Nashville, I set my sights on New York City. However, fate had other plans. I had a date with a girl named Crystal; a few months later I ended up moving into her St. Louis home.

We started a family the next year and I co-founded a production company that started producing *The Darryn Yates Show*. It was a podcast, web series, morning-drive radio show, and a local TV show.

This entertainment journey was an awesome ride. But with a growing family and not getting a big break, I figured it was time to grow up and get a regular job.

However, I absolutely hated having a boss, helping someone else's vision happen, being told what I was worth, and I hated the idea of giving up on my real dreams and passions. So, I quit, or I was fired at least 12 times.

I researched and soul-searched in a way I had never done before. This was for survival, for happiness, to be fully present with my wife and kids. The dreams I gave up on, the entertainment journey I was ashamed of for years...I realized was just the foundation of something bigger. My dreams were in entertainment, but my purpose and my calling was to help inspire others to fully maximize their potential.

I also had another huge realization. Back then it was all about getting noticed or signed by a gatekeeper. But in today's online marketing world, the gatekeepers have been eliminated.

It is about leaning into your story, personality, and vision. You must find something that you love doing so much that you will power through the resistance: your cynical & negative inner circles, a debilitating traditional fixed mindset, haters, and stable jobs that make you miserable and that force you to give up on your REAL vision of what you want your life to be.

The crazy journey of chasing my dreams was the scenic route that I needed to take. I even needed to hit rock bottom to reset the fire, passion, and hunger to want to bounce back and crush it. Being at rock bottom is also evidence that we care, and we want more. We know something just isn't quite right. Difficult times often tell us that we are closer than we think to figuring it out.

I encourage those of you who are going through any kind of difficult time... remember that as long as you don't stop and you keep tweaking, learning, and grinding...you will figure it out. Even if you don't capture the main goal you set out to, if you just stay on the journey... all of your experiences and the people you meet along the way... what you end up doing is probably going to be pretty sweet and very much related to that main goal. Keep going, be consistent, follow your heart, and don't be afraid to do it alone for a bit if needed.

Once I started telling my story of hitting rock bottom, the response was incredible. People told me how inspired they were and wanted me to help them. My one-on-one coaching business started in a very organic way.

After a year of doing this, I started putting a team together to help me transition to an online coaching program. I officially gave up the good to go for the great. I have also returned to my crazy cool edgy variety show, *The Darryn Yates Show.*

When you take massive action to change your life, many that you thought were on your side...will not be. Embrace this and know you are on the right path. When you are loved or hated, know you're onto something. People are going to judge you no matter what you do, so you might as well live the life you know you're capable of, the life you know you deserve.

Thank you for your time and go live those dreams.

Reveal your rockstar, and answer the following questions...

What dream or inner purpose are you feeling, right now?

_____

_____

_____

_____

What story can you share? Brainstorm a list of wonderful things you've accomplished and hardships you've overcome.

_____

_____

_____

_____

What's one thing you can do today that can make your inner passion come alive?

_____

_____

_____

_____

About The Author

Darryn Yates grew up in Granite City IL, near St. Louis MO. He moved to southern CA at age 20 to live his dream in rock music. On Tracy Lane is the all-original rock band Darryn started in Los Angeles. OTL opened for several national acts, toured the US, went overseas to play for the US troops and did several music videos including one with actress Lacey Chabert.

Darryn moved to Nashville TN and licensed over 15 of his songs to TV, film, and commercials. Nearly 2 years later he met his future wife, Crystal, and moved into her St. Louis home. They started a family the next year and Darryn started doing The Darryn Yates Show. It was a podcast, web series, morning-drive radio show, and local TV show.

With a growing family and Darryn not getting a big break, he entered the corporate world. He butted heads with bosses and quit or got fired at least 12 times. Darryn hit rock bottom in early 2019 and had 2 choices: stay on a dark path or bounce back and crush it. He chose the latter.

Darryn Yates helps people lean into what they really want to do. He is the host of The Darryn Yates Show and the singer/songwriter of On Tracy Lane.

AUTHOR CONTACT INFORMATION

Darryn Yates, *Personal Branding Coach & Host of the Darryn Yates Show*
Website: www.DarrynYates.com
Linkedin: https://www.linkedin.com/in/the-darryn-yates-show-b5a507b/
Email: darryn@leaninanddominate.com
Tiktok: tiktok.com/@thedarrynyatesshow
YouTube: youtube.com/darrynyates
Instagram: instagram.com/thedarrynyatesshow
Instagram: @DarrynYates

CHAPTER 32

WINNER'S MINDSET:
ON + OFF THE FIELD

By Danielle Fagan

"Most coaches and athletes know there are life lessons from playing the sport. As an accomplished coach and athlete, herself, Danielle takes the lessons on the field and teaches people how to apply them off the field."

— Cara Bradley, Mental Fitness Coach and author of On The Verge: Wake up, Show up and Shine.

BE PREPARED
On The Field

I love coaching. I lie awake at night reviewing checklists in my head, making sure I did everything possible to prepare my team to succeed. I expect to win. I am passionate. I love coaching not just because I am competitive, but because I care so much: about the players, the team and how our successes and failures will translate into lessons they can use in life, jobs, relationships. We had routines. We were consistent. We controlled the controllables so even if something changed in our plan, we could adjust without fail.

We arrived at the State Semi-Final game where a dense fog hung ominously over parts of the turf. There were moments I could not see the ball, the teams, the field. I could only hear the players shouting, the referee's whistle and the roar of the crowd from the stands across the field. We won that night because we were ready for anything, and not even the fog could stop us.

Off The Field

- Prepare so you can anticipate, react and deal with any situation. Preparation makes it easier to respond to unpredictability.

- Part of preparation is knowing what you can control and focusing on that. We can control our expectations, effort, attitude, communication and how we prepare.

- Implement a routine, create a plan and be consistent. It will increase productivity, reduce stress, and improve your chances at success.

KNOW YOUR ROLE
On The Field

Some players are goal-scorers, some are ball-winners. Some rally the team from the bench. Every player has a role and responsibility. There are starters, superstars, and substitutes. There are only 11 positions on the field, a time limit on the game and not everyone can be captain. Yet every member has something to contribute and an opportunity to lead.

I called a substitute to my side. I told her, "Get the ball to Kim. Just find her when you win the ball. You are a ball winner. Win the ball. Find Kim's feet. That's your job." She entered the game. And not a minute passed before she intercepted the ball and played a perfect pass to Kim who slotted the ball past the goalkeeper for the game-winning goal. She did her part and helped us win.

Off The Field

- Know your strengths and when and where to use them.

- Recognize when it makes sense to rely on others who are more experienced or proficient.

- Discover the best ways you can contribute; when to lead and when to follow. Not everyone can be in charge, but everyone wins when you support the leaders and work together.

EVERYONE CARRIES EQUIPMENT
On The Field

My goal was to create a family atmosphere and develop trust, loyalty, and friendship in a competitive and challenging environment that pushed players beyond their perceived limits. I eliminated the rule that freshmen had to carry equipment. Team chemistry was paramount to our success. Everyone carried equipment: Captains, Seniors, everyone. We won a lot of games, but the strongest bonds were forged when we lost or had to deal with adversity.

One of our players was whisked out of school just before practice started so she could get to the hospital to say goodbye to her dad whom doctors said only had a few hours to live. Reluctant to start practice and wondering how to support their teammate, the players created a giant heart on the field with their bodies and a "T" in the middle. They snapped the picture and texted it to her. Happy ending: her dad miraculously recovered.

Off The Field

- Win and lose together.

- Look for ways to support others.

- What's important in the moment may be the biggest win.

NEXT FIVE
On The Field

The team and I would constantly shout, "Next Five!" It meant no matter what happens: miss a tackle, score a goal, be sure to focus for the next five minutes after every play and always know the score. There are no timeouts in soccer, so we created a way to communicate in the flow of the game.

It was cold and raining. We had a goal called back as one of our players was called offside. We played on and went down 1-0. At the start of the second half, shouting "Next Five!" was key and set the tone for the rest of the game. Just after kick-off, the opponent was on a breakaway, our keeper came out and deflected the shot back at the opponent who shot again and hit the crossbar. The rebound back to the opponent gave her a clear shot at the open goal. She struck the ball and out of nowhere came our outside back to clear the ball off the goal line. We tied the game shortly thereafter and then went ahead 2-1. The opponent quickly equalized 2-2. With minutes remaining on the clock, we earned a corner kick. The kick soared in front of their goal and deflected to a midfielder who was in perfect position to put the ball in the back of the next to seal the win 3-2.

Off The Field

- There are no timeouts in life. It keeps moving and you cannot stop it, but you can break it up into shorter periods of time to help you stay focused.

- Break down challenging moments and tasks into smaller pieces.

- Constantly re-focus every time there is a new challenge and never give up.

24 HOUR RULE
On The Field

My team had a very explicit rule. Celebrate a victory and suffer a loss for no longer than 24 hours. I wanted them to experience it and move on, win or lose.

With about two minutes left in double overtime we were knotted at 0-0. We had momentum. Or so I thought as one of our center backs lunged for the ball and the speedy opponent deftly dribbled by her towards our goal and hammered home the game winner. One minute we were tied and the next the game was over. After the game I told the players: "We have 24 hours to be upset, angry and frustrated."

The next day at practice our focus was on the next game. We went on an 18-game winning streak and won the state championship. Would we have been state champs had we been so focused on our loss? One will never know, but I would argue we gave ourselves a better chance by moving on quickly from the loss.

Off The Field

- Celebrate your wins in life but do it briefly so you can find a new challenge.

- Do whatever you have to do to deal with the losses in life so you can start fresh the next day. My team wrote down all the mistakes they made in the game and then everyone put them through a paper shredder in the team room. Did the mistakes go away? No, but they were able to move on to the next game and win.

- The positives and the negatives are always going to influence you. It is how you respond to the wins and losses that keeps you on the path to success.

Apply the winner mindset in your life, and answer the following questions...

What ways can you prepare ahead of time? What are you in control of?

_____

_____

_____

_____

How can you be a team player? What are your strengths and weaknesses? How can you contribute?

_____

_____

_____

_____

How can you support others? How will you manage breakdowns? How will you celebrate the wins?

_____

_____

_____

_____

ABOUT THE AUTHOR

Danielle Fagan is a licensed soccer coach and consultant. A passionate coach for over 25 years, she creates champions in sports, business, wellness, and life using a winner's mindset.

Danielle earned a BA and MBA from Villanova University, where she captained the women's soccer and softball teams and was an assistant soccer and strength coach. Danielle teaches athletes and coaches to achieve peak performance and build successful teams and leaders using life lessons from sports.

AUTHOR CONTACT INFORMATION

Danielle Fagan, *Licensed soccer coach and consultant*
Website: www.soccerdcf.com
Email: soccerdcf@yahoo.com
Social: IG/Twitter/Facebook @soccerdcf
Website: https://daniellefagancoaching.godaddysites.com
Phone: 610-505-5567

CHAPTER 33

POSITION OF CONTROL - MASTERING THE ZORRO CIRCLE

By David Medansky

"If you can't explain it simply, do it simply, design it simply, it is because you don't understand it well enough."

— Albert Einstein

What is the Zorro Circle, you might be wondering?

The Zorro Circle is a metaphor to limit your focus to master small, manageable goals, so later you can then expand the scope of your ability and capability. In the movie, The Mask of Zorro Alejandro - Zorro (played by Antonio Banderas) is a broken man. That is because as a young man, his ambition to fight villains and right the injustices in the world far exceeded his knowledge and skill set. After many attempts and many failures, Alejandro, frustrated, feels disillusioned and powerless. He surrenders to alcohol, falls into a deep despair, and loses his confidence.

Fortunately for Alejandro, he meets a mentor, Don Diego (played by Anthony Hopkins), an aging sword master. It is Don Diego who helps Alejandro regain his confidence by helping him gain a sense of control, giving him back his focus, conviction, and perseverance.

When Zorro first started, he had no focus and no sense of control. He wants to do too much to quickly. However, he does not know where to start. This is how many people who want to lose weight feel. They want to do too much too quickly. They are unaware of how to start to improve their eating habits. It can be daunting and overwhelming. Does it sound familiar?

There is a scene in the movie where Zorro's training commences when Don Diego places Zorro in a small training circle. Don Diego tells Zorro, "This is called a training circle, a master's wheel. This circle will be your world, your whole life, until I tell you otherwise. There is nothing outside of it…As your skill with the sword improves, you will progress to a larger circle…"

The small circle is for Zorro to control. A simple path to follow, he must master what is inside the circle before he can expand it or move on to the next circle. This is what you must do to improve and master your daily eating habits. You must master one circle at a time. For instance, the first and most important daily eating habit you must master is to drink an adequate amount of pure water. This is the foundation of all healthy weight loss and healthy lifestyle.

Once Alejandro mastered control of that small circle, Don Diego slowly started to expand his circle allowing him to attempt bigger and bigger feats, which one by one, Zorro achieves.

Likewise, as you master drinking an adequate amount of pure water each day, then you can move on to the next circle, which is avoiding all processed and manufactured food products. And, once you have mastered avoiding all processed and manufactured food products, then you move onto eating organic, whole, or holistic foods.

As Zorro gained more confidence, he learned how to command his emotions and utilize his skills. None of Zorro's achievements would have been possible had he not first been able to master that small circle. Similarly, what this means for you is it will be difficult, if not impossible, for you to achieve and maintain healthy weight loss if you do not first master being able to drink an adequate amount of pure water and control your emotions.

Before Alejandro mastered the small circle, he had no command over his emotions, no sense of his own skill, no real faith in his ability to accomplish a goal. And, worst of all, no feeling of control over his fate.

Do you feel this way too? That you have no control over your emotions, no sense of skill of how to eat healthy, or what it means to eat healthy, no real faith in your ability to accomplish your weight loss goal? And no feeling of being able to control your daily eating habits to lose weight? Do you fail to make it to even the second Zorro circle (avoid processed and manufactured foods) because your cravings sabotage you?

The lesson of the story of the Zorro circle is this: to achieve anything in life you need to focus your efforts on small, manageable tasks, which once accomplished, gives a sense of control. This builds confidence. As your confidence grows, so will your desire to continue. By first limiting the extent of your weight-loss efforts, then watching those efforts have an intended effect, you gain knowledge and confidence to expand the circle, mastering larger and larger areas. Before long, you will change your daily eating habits, lose weight, feel better, improve your overall health, and want to do more.

I encounter clients who struggle taking charge of their own eating behaviors and lifestyles. The Zorro circle helps them take a simple path to accomplish their weight loss success.

Your Zorro Circle: The 9 Fundamental Principles for Healthy Weight Loss

1. Drink an adequate amount (64 ounces or more) of pure water each day.

2. Avoid processed and manufactured foods also known as edible products.

3. Eat organic, holistic/whole foods, mostly plants.\

4. Eat slowly.

5. Eat small portions.

6. Get adequate sleep.

7. Focus on the food you eat by eliminating distractions that can cause "mindless" eating.

8. Give your body 12 to 14 hours each day to digest and process the food you consume.

9. Keep a positive mindset by focusing on the foods you should eat that are healthy rather than the edible products you crave that are known to be unhealthy. What you focus on expands.

MASTERING THE ZORRO CIRCLE
AS IT APPLIES TO HEALTHY WEIGHT LOSS

Knowing what to do to lose weight is a good start. Changing and improving daily habits is a key component of your weight loss success and healthy weight management. You don't need to modify all your bad habits at one time to significantly improve your life. Just as Alejandro had grand intentions, we all start with grand intentions to lose weight. However, we are overcome by the irresistible call of unhealthy foods and beverages. The instant gratification and comfort, not to mention the convenience, of these highly processed foods and artificially sweetened beverages overwhelms our sense and are hard to resist. This is why it is important to master a small circle, so we learn to control our emotions as it relates to food. Achieving your healthy and sustainable weight is possible and you too can do it.

Master the Zorro Circle, and answer the following questions…

What areas do you like to focus and control? And why?

_____

_____

_____

_____

How would your life be different if you retained focus and mastered control?

_____

_____

_____

_____

What is one area you can work on right now to apply the Zorro circle?

_____

_____

_____

_____

ABOUT THE AUTHOR

David Medansky, The Anti-Diet Advocate, is a former divorce attorney and award-winning international bestselling author. David helps people stop losing money on diets because diets are designed to fail.

David struggled with his own weight issues until July of 2016 when his doctor told him to lose weight or find a new doctor. He understands your frustrations. David was able to shed 50 pounds, almost 25 percent of his total body weight.

Now he wants to teach you how to eat healthier so you can have more energy, feel better, and improve your overall health without having to order special meals, purchase diet supplements or products, without having to count calories and without having to follow a specific exercise program. If you're struggling to reduce weight or keep it off, *David's 9 Fundamental Must Have Principles for Healthy Weight Loss* is a good place to start your weight loss journey.

AUTHOR CONTACT INFORMATION

David Medansky, *The Anti-Diet Advocate*
You can learn more at www.AntiDietAdvocate.com

THE 5 GOLDEN RULES OF SALES TO GET PEOPLE TO TAKE ACTION

By Mike Lamothe

"Love people enough to tell the truth even when it isn't pretty"

— Mike Lamothe

"Sales is where love and self-respect meet." I often repeat this quote I heard some time ago.

What this means to me is: "Loving people enough to tell them the truth and respecting yourself enough to not let BS slide."

––––––

A client, Heather, came to me with a big problem of calls taking too long and prospects still needing to "think about it." As part of our coaching sessions, I brought the *5 Sales Killers* to her attention.

Now, I'll identify each Sales Killer and the Rule that handles it.

RULE #1: BE OUTCOME-INDEPENDENT

Sales Killer #1: Neediness - needing the sale or needing people to like you.

Heather was trying too hard to get rapport because she needed people to like her and also "needed" the sale. This is gross. People sense when all you want is a sale, and it repels them. They won't trust you and without trust they can't buy. Rapport-seeking and wanting others to like you creates doubt in the prospect's mind.

As soon as you let go of the outcome your ability to influence and enroll clients doubles. You have nothing to prove, so you won't go into convincing mode (which conveys neediness). You will be able to speak your truth because you are not worried about blowing the sale.

You will finally be free on the calls to be yourself with no hidden agenda. You are there to get to the truth and hold up the mirror so people can see their real situation. Some people won't like what they see and might take it out on you. That's OK. You need to say what they need to hear, not what they want to hear.

Speaking from certainty and your truth is a superpower.

RULE #2: GET SPECIFIC

Sales Killer #2: Staying on the surface

The problem with this is people never see the true severity of their problems. And most of us downplay our problems, "it's not that bad," etc. Don't let vague answers slide. Make them answer the question until you completely understand their situation.

Example if they say, "Oh man, it is so bad." I have no idea what that means. So, I would say something like, "When you say it is so bad, what does that look like specifically?" or "what does that mean specifically?" or "how is that affecting you personally?"

Sometimes, after you ask a question, they go into a long story and never answer you. So, you have to say, "OK got ya," and then ask the same question again. *Get specific.*

RULE #3: DON'T HIDE BEHIND NICE

Sales Killer #3: Not Challenging People

Being able to challenge and collide with limiting beliefs is a must. That is the only way you can help people have a breakthrough or huge shift so they can and will take action. People always say, "I don't want to be mean, I want to be nice." So, they never call people out. Then people don't sign up and will most likely die with the same problem. I don't think that is very nice.

I usually say the most selfish thing you can do is be nice and not say anything. It means your need to be comfortable is more important than helping people shift. That means they will continue to suffer.

> *"There are no such thing as people pleasers, only conflict avoiders"* - Danielle K. White

Along these lines, I say, "Love people enough to tell them the truth, especially when it isn't pretty."

RULE #4: DON'T GET SOLD

Sales Killer #4: Getting sold on the clients' stories

People will tell you all their sob stories about how they are broke or all these bad things that happen to them. You have to be able to hear them without feeling bad for them (no, sympathy doesn't help them).

Your certainty about your program has to be higher than their certainty about their doubts. People have been telling themselves these stories for so long they believe them to be the truth.

Don't get sold on them.

Those reasons they give you are the exact reasons why they need to do something about it and why they need you. Remember: All the things they tell you are not the problem. They are symptoms of a bigger problem.

RULE #5: OWN THE FRAME OR END THE CALL

Sales Killer #5: Not Having Frame Control

If you don't own the frame, they will never enroll into your program. Also, you want clients that can follow. If people have to control everything and can't follow, they are going to be nightmare clients. They will always know better, and all you will hear is "Ya, but…"

Better to call them out and say, "During this call, all you have been doing is bucking, and you seem to want to control the call." That is a red flag for me that this person might not be very coachable. If you can't be the lead on a call, then coaching could be a nightmare.

One approach could be: "You seem to know a lot. Why do you think you haven't been able to *[the outcome they want]?"*

This kind of come-to-Jesus talk might make them aware and be open to listening and being led. If it doesn't, do yourself and the other person a favor and end the call.

Now there is a caveat here, and it has to do with buyer sophistication. The higher the buyer sophistication, the more skills you need with the framing. For those who have higher buyer sophistication, you need to be careful about how you do your framing.

Do you want to know more about advanced frame control? Get my free video at https://enrollingmastery.com/frame-control-formula

It is so important that you don't let just anybody into your program. There are more important things than bringing in money.

Follow these 5 rules and your ability to sell and get people to take action will skyrocket.

Let's end the sales killers to your business, and answer the following questions...

In what ways can you speak from certainty and share your truth?

_____

_____

_____

_____

How can you frame the call and be in control?

_____

_____

_____

_____

What are the 5 Sales Killers related to how you conduct your business? And how can you overcome them?

_____

_____

_____

_____

About The Author

Coaches: Do you want to increase your enrollment rate by 60%? Add an extra $60,000 in the next 90 Days Guaranteed. Work with Mike Lamothe, Founder of Enrolling Mastery. Mike helps clients like Daniela go from a 3% enrollment rate to a 60% enrollment rate. Mike listened to her calls and helped her transform her whole approach. He showed her how to turn her calls into clients. Trained in NLP, Mike has also sold over $50 million in products and coaching in various industries.

AUTHOR CONTACT INFORMATION

Mike Lamothe, *Sales Trainer for Coaches*
Website: EnrollingMastery.com
Email: mike@enrollingmastery.com
Facebook: FB.com/enrollingmastery
LinkedIn: https://www.linkedin.com/in/michaellamothe/

CHAPTER 35

SUCCESS OR FAILURE
THE CHOICE IS YOURS!

By Tom Loegering and TJ Loegering

"Success = getting what you want.
Happiness = wanting what you get!"

— Tom Loegering

My goal is to help people get on the right path to success. Whether you desire to start a new business or non-profit, or if you are just seeking self-improvement, my purpose is to get you to start by developing goals, building plans, then implement, analyze, correct, and to continuously repeat this process.

Once you make the decision to get started, you begin developing your vision. This sets in motion the motivation necessary to establish goals. This, in turn, gives you renewed energy and allows you to achieve all you can conceive. Visualize your goal, spend part of each day writing down the overview of your plan, and then incorporate it into your business plan and set up an organization chart. Begin to operate as an income-producing company designed for success. You will reach your goals. It gets easier over time, especially when you find out who you are, what you want, and realize that happiness comes from giving to causes that you believe in.

Sometime after I reached my first goal and during my first retirement, I decided I needed to put my next goals onto paper. But taking heed of my father's advice, I decided to become a realtor because of the ease of entry and the only risk was my time. At the time I would have liked to have the advice I am giving here.

"Operate yourself like a business. Develop an organization chart and a business plan. Visualize the money and lifestyle you want."

When I entered the real estate business, I got started without a proper business plan and organization chart, but we got started! We wrote down the amount of money we wanted not realizing the pressures of the change in lifestyle that we might encounter. We developed a strategy that was designed to acquire properties for clients, sometimes people we didn't even know. We then found programs sponsored by the government that wanted to put people in their own homes, even if they had no down payment or closing costs. We found a large group of clientele willing to purchase a property under these government programs. These were programs designed to help people who had integrity and willingness to pay off their loans, not programs to help people who only have a need.

We developed a ten-year program to make 10 people millionaires and, in the process, become one ourselves. It wasn't necessary to earn enough income to put $100,000 cash in the bank each year to reach our goal. Purchasing an appreciating property will shelter income and increase net worth. The plan was developed to use as many methods to purchase property as possible. We were not flippers to buy, fix, and sell properties. We bought, fixed up, refinanced, exchanged, and repeated.

Learning about business cycles is important so you can plan for the cycle you are in. Excess leads to collapse. Collapse then leads to recovery which in turn leads to excesses. That's the cycle. This is the repeating pattern that will run until the government runs out of ink and paper to print money or where the people refuse to accept paper money. During one of these down cycles when bank loans were very difficult to acquire, we developed more than 30 different methods to acquire real estate. The last choice was to use our own cash. These methods are directly born from defining and planning to reach goals.

To have balance in my life I needed to coordinate these seven parts of life in developing my goals:

- *Personal:* One of the true joys we get from life is when we can help others. GPS was conceived as a way to open up new vistas and expose students to opportunities they might not otherwise have experienced.

- *Financial:* GPS provided a new source of revenue for Sun City Country Club. Providing free golf to students who complete the program directly enhanced the club revenue in green fees received from the adults accompanying the students, as well as ancillary revenue from merchandise, food, and beverage sales.

- *Family:* GPS became part of our extended family. Many like-minded people became enthusiastic volunteers. Mentoring students created relationships that will last a lifetime. GPS has also enhanced and strengthened family relationships between students and parents by providing a shared activity.

- *Physical:* Part of the mission of GPS is to promote physical fitness. To get students off the couch, their heads out of video games, and get them outside engaging in healthy physical activity.

- *Community:* GPS offers a cost-free program to the community called Free Family Fun-Day once a month. We believe that by making a difference in the lives of the students and their families, we are making our communities a better place to live.

- *Professional:* GPS has built its foundation as a 501-c-3, including Board of Directors, a formal business plan and our policies and procedures to ensure a solid base to grow from.

- *Spiritual:* "Do unto others as you would have them do unto you," is, in one form or another, found in every religion of the world. We have been very fortunate in our lives and GPS is our attempt to 'pay it back/forward'. Our goal is to do well in our business so we can do good in our community!

HOW I PURSUED MY PASSION (And how you can too) provides an example of how I used these principles to create a successful and rewarding business. But, as stated, there is more to success than a successful business. I have always wanted to give back; to pay it forward. In 2014 I had an "aha" moment. When I retired for the seventh time and moved to Sun City, Arizona, I didn't just "drop out." I got involved in the community. The Sun City Country Club was hemorrhaging money and about to close. This club has been a vital asset to the community since 1966 and it would have left a hole in the community if it went out of business. So, we purchased it. Now I was the owner of a struggling golf course that was operating in the red. About that same time, I was also on the Peoria Education Foundation Board of Directors and one of my responsibilities was to vote on "Against All Odds" scholarships for students who overcame health issues, language barriers, family tragedies and financial hardships with courage and fortitude. While reading over one of the applications I was struck by the idea "Could it be possible to merge these two completely different realms and benefit both kids and golf?" As this idea started to congeal, I began to see an image of kids learning golf and then bringing their families to play golf. I realized I could offer the kids free playing privileges at the golf course when they played with a paying adult.

This would not only help my community by promoting family unity and strengthening the family bond but would enhance the revenue of my golf club by bringing new golfers to the course. Out of this "aha" moment the Golf Program in Schools (GPS) was born.

Golf Program in Schools provides lessons to students during their regularly scheduled physical education classes at no cost to the student or the school; thus, eliminating all socioeconomic limitations. During the one-week program certified GPS or PGA instructors teach students *(G)Grip, (P)posture, and (S)Swing* along with golf course etiquette – courtesy and respect for themselves, other students and other golfers on the course.

As part of the one-week program, students are invited to attend a field trip to the golf course to learn and practice chipping, putting and driving. Upon completion of the program students that complete our survey are provided free golf (with a paying adult) until they graduate from high school. Students may also opt for further instruction in our GPS Academy. The GPS Academy provides group and individual lessons at family-affordable pricing. In the four years we operated GPS we have reached over 30,000 students. Many testimonials and Awards have shown the effect this program has had on students' lives. Not only that, but the revenue at our golf course has also increased 51% over the last 5 years.

As I write this the trend for 2021 continues to show increased revenue and rounds and we anticipate the golf course operating at a "PROFIT" for the first time in many years. The future for GPS is great as this business model is scalable for many other communities, families, kids and golf courses. The principles I used to create and operate my successful real estate business were the same principles I used to create GPS. These are the principles described here. Unlike my real estate business GPS is a 501(c) 3 non-profit. But it doesn't matter whether your goal is a for-profit or non- profit, or whether you just want to be organized and change the direction your life is traveling. The principles given here work if you Do and can help you reach your goals.

I wrote my book, "Success or Failure, The Choice is Yours," after extensive research and observations about what we need to get the most out of our lives. After all, you only have one life to live. Life is not a dress rehearsal. Make the most of it! Click your "start button" and begin the journey to a happy, healthy and productive life so you don't retire *P.O.O.R.* - Person that Overlooks Opportunity Regularly.

The first step on your journey is to recognize where you are now. You can't make a map to a successful destination until you know your starting point. Next, understand that the decisions you made in the past brought you to where you are now, including mental and physical health, as well as personal finances. Examining why you made poor decisions in the past can give you the insight that will allow you to regain control of your life.

If you discover the "why" you can find the "way." Remember, YOU ARE IN CHARGE! One important exercise is to begin, look at obstacles as opportunities. Know, you are a business and in control of your life. To operate at a profit, you must learn to live your life well as a productive person and business so you can do well for yourself and Good in your communities.

Pursuing happiness is our goal, but as Professor Adam Grant suggests that our quest for happiness might be a recipe for misery. Professor Grant believes that happiness can only be successfully pursued indirectly. It's a by-product of doing meaningful things that tell us our lives stand for something that benefits others. This makes us feel good about ourselves which is what happiness is all about. Do well in the business of running your life so you can do good for others.

Remember:

Success = getting what you want.
Happiness = wanting what you get!

Pursue your happiness and passions, and answer the following questions...

How will you balance the seven areas (Personal, Financial, Family, Physical, Community, Professional & Spiritual) in your life?

_____

_____

_____

_____

Describe your passion and what it means to you...

_____

_____

_____

_____

Create a road map to success! Outline the beginning steps to get started....

_____

_____

_____

_____

ABOUT THE AUTHORS

After being born in Minnesota, Tom moved to Southern California. After serving two terms in the army working as a cryptographer for NSA, he started his 55-year career path assisting his father in all phases of residential and commercial property construction and property management in Southern California.

He attended California State University, Long Beach with a focus in Business and Finance. After receiving his contractor's license, he started Loegering Management in 1969. Tom spent 27 years running the company, and during that time was awarded a Certified Property Manager designation enabling him to maximize investment returns on over 5000 residential units.

Since 1995, Tom has acted in consulting and advisory capacities for public and private real estate investment trusts. He was awarded a contract in response to a Request for Proposal from the State of California and Caltrans Housing and Community Development and was responsible for a 5-year contract relating to the housing needs for 3500 families caused by the construction of the Century Freeway in Southern California.

Tom was the founder of an IRA Management Company which grew to have 650 million dollars under management in the 3 years before it was sold, was the Owner and Broker for Accura Escrow Company and Effective Funding Mortgage Company. Tom also started the first All-Internet Building in Los Angeles and raised the income over 50% in one year.

Tom moved to Sun City, Arizona in 2005. In 2007 he became the CEO for the family-owned Sun City Country Club, a 127-acre, 18-hole championship golf course and country club. He and his staff are currently on track to re-establishing this historically significant golf club's former premiere status.

Tom became a Certified Mentor for SCORE, an organization which counsels Americans in Small Business and was named Rookie of the Year in 2008. He has served 3 years on the Recreation Center of Sun City's Board of Directors and served on the Outreach and Communications committee. This organization oversees 90 million dollars in assets with a 17 million dollar per year budget.

Tom has also authored a book entitled "Success or Failure – The Choice is Yours" and has written and taught several courses for the Department of Real Estate as a Founding Member of the Property Management Section of the National Association of Realtors. Tom was on the Board of Governors of the Arizona Golf Association. He received the 2012 citizen of the year for Sun City and is a member of Leadership West class XX and a Founding member of Leadership West Alumni Association. Tom is a member of Cohort 14 Goldman Sachs SB10k program and received Special Recognition from Babson College in 2015.

Tom served 9 years on the Board of Directors for the Peoria Chamber of Commerce and is on the Board of Directors of the Peoria Education Foundation. Tom is the Founder and Chairman of Golf Program in Schools, Inc or GPS Introducing 30,500, 5-9th grade students to golfs life's lessons while finding their path to scholarships, job and career opportunities in golf.

When not acting as CEO, Chairman, Managing Director, Mentor or participating in volunteer activities by helping victims of domestic violence at Eve's Place or helping kids with autism. Tom and Suzanne have traveled on their Motorcycle enjoying their adventures. They have traveled in the U.S., Mexico, Europe, New Zealand, and Australia.

AUTHOR CONTACT INFORMATION

Tom Loegering, *Owner Sun City Country Club, Chairman of Golf Program in Schools*
Website: https://golfps.org/
Email: tom@suncitycountryclub.org
Linkedin: https://www.linkedin.com/in/tom-loegering-8576a39/

PILLAR 4

IMPACT

CHAPTER 36

FOUR FUTURES, ONE CHOICE!

"The future depends on what we do in the present."

— *Mahatma Gandhi*

I want you to take a moment and think of your life as divided into three intertwined parts: the past, the present, and the future. All three of these concepts play an active role in your everyday decision-making and response to the world around you. Your experience from a past event can dictate your present and future responses. Maybe you were once in a relationship that ended badly, and you were hurt by the person you loved. As a result, today you may be guarded and defensive. You may even avoid getting into another relationship, because of your fear of future pain.

Many people choose to live in the past and end up stuck there, while others worry obsessively about the future. Very few people take the time to live in the present and be mindful of their actions and emotions. They get caught up thinking about would-have, could-have, should-have regrets for things that have already happened and can't be undone. I've been there, too. I've made poor decisions. I've said things out of ignorance, anger, fear, and shame. But I've learned from those experiences and adjusted my life accordingly. Who I was at eighteen years old, a naive boy who got his girlfriend pregnant is no longer the man I am today. I have done the work to let go of the past, forgive, and realize every new day is a unique experience and not an experience from my past.

We carry our past into our future, which is why the present is truly a gift. Being in the present requires you to appreciate where you are, what you have, and who is with you at the moment.

What if you woke up every morning with a clean slate to begin again?

Because you do! That is what intentional living is about, being present in the now, not regretting what happened yesterday, and not worrying about tomorrow, but just focusing on today!

My beloved grandmother, who is currently 94, wakes up every morning with a smile on her face, always in a state of happiness. People always ask her, *"Rose, how are you always so happy?"* She replies with enthusiasm, *"I woke up."* My grandmother lives in a place of gratitude, grateful that she is able to spend another day around her family and friends. So, I ask you, *Are you waking up grateful every day?*

Your tight grip on the past influences your decision, as do your worry and fear of the future. You need to choose to let go and use what you have learned so far in this book. Dive deep into what you want. Start making a positive impact on your life! Right now, you have four choices that will create a difference over the next twelve months in your life. These choices will impact you today, tomorrow, and years from now.

You can take path one and slide down the slippery slope of being a victim with the *"Why me?"* mindset. You can take path two and choose to live your life as-is because you've made it this far and are *"Okay"* with it. Path three relies on *"just winging it,"* where you *"Try"* to make a difference in your life with no definite plan of action.

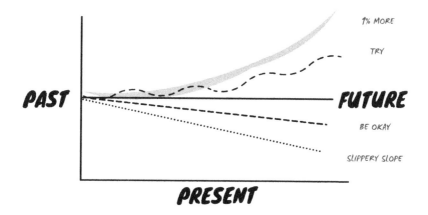

Or you can choose path four, apply what you have learned, and live intentionally to create an extraordinary life by doing *1% More!*

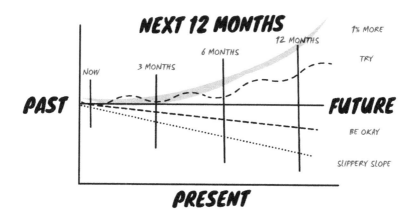

The longer you wait the harder it will become for you to move away from the past and begin creating a future you love. A gap will begin to grow as time goes on separating you further and further from creating and living your dream! I ask, *Why waste any more time?*

Ask yourself, *How would I feel if I had a fulfilled life? How would I feel to have less worry and anxiety? How would I envision my life if I could no longer be stuck?*

Your future is open to unlimited possibilities. Once you become present in the moment and take action, the constraints of the past will slowly disappear. You will begin to realize that anything is possible. Let yourself be vulnerable, take a step into the unknown, and release the past. Your life is unique, so fill it with passion and purpose and embrace the knowledge you have gained from this book and create a lifestyle of *1% More!*

CHAPTER 37

THE HIDDEN FORCE WITHIN!

*Realize that enough hidden strength lies within you
to overcome all obstacles and temptations.
Bring forth that indomitable power and energy.*

*— Paramahansa Yogananda,
Indian Hindu monk, yogi and guru*

Throughout this book, you have been shown the way with easy-to-apply and straightforward strategies that will allow you to layout the road map that takes you from *"You Are Here"* to your destination of success and happiness by just applying *1% More* to your life.

You have been given a choice; to continue down the same path and be *"okay"* or believe in yourself and take action to transform. It is time to choose your new adventure and impact the world. The time for you to shine is now!

If you have chosen to continue down the same old path, you may want to read through this book again and see what else may be missing from your life or seek guidance from one of the fantastic coaches listed within these pages.

If you have chosen the path of *1% More*, I welcome you to the new opportunities that lie ahead.

You should feel honored by your choice because you are stepping into the space of a leader, a person who will be inspiring and courageous, and who will motivate others to follow in your footsteps for years to come. You may be thinking, *"Me a leader?"* Yes, you! You hold the power and force within you.

You now have many tools to begin your journey to learn about and practice self-awareness, growth, and taking action. You are the "Hidden Force," the mysterious energy with unlimited abilities and knowledge to create an extraordinary life. Adding the concept of *1% More* into existence along with your inner power, your *F.O.R.C.E.*™ will cause a ripple effect of positive energy to overcome any challenges you face.

The word *F.O.R.C.E.*™ stands for *Functioning Optimally Regardless of Challenges Encountered.* Where you once lacked the knowledge and resources, you now can make wiser and intentional decisions that can and will have a more significant impact on your life. You will now function on a higher mental, physical and spiritual level than you have ever done before. You'll see things from a new perspective, think more clearly, and be in tune with your intuition. Listen carefully to that intuition, let it guide you, and overcome the obstacles that stand before you.

At times, becoming a leader is by choice; other times, the role is forced upon you. You may need to make unexpected and tough decisions, as I did recently with my father's passing and with many other events before that. Even though I was outside my comfort zone, I rose to the occasion with each one, and so can you!

To grow as a leader, we need to recognize our strengths, weaknesses, and everything else in between. We all have two types of strengths, natural and hidden. Natural strengths are talents, knowledge, and abilities you already possess and come quickly to you. Hidden strengths are things you didn't realize you were good at or could develop to enhance your potential.

Thuy Sindell and Milo Sindell, authors of Hidden Strengths: Unleashing the Crucial Leadership Skills You Already Have, share that people only focus on the top 20% of their natural strength, leaving so much potential behind. Knowing what you are good at and focusing on these strengths is useful but ignores the unknown possibilities and potential that exist.

Your middle set of skills *(Hidden Strengths)* is untapped potential and can, in time, develop into powerful strengths. Examples of these hidden strengths are emotional control, resilience, self-confidence, listening, teamwork, entrepreneurship, and delegation, to name a few. To harness the power of these forces, you must first recognize what your natural strengths are and those that need improvement. Second, identify which hidden strength you want to focus on, according to your goals. Third, practice, practice, practice! With practice, your hidden strength evolves into a natural force.

Remember, leaders are not born; they are made! Anyone can learn to lead. Begin by stepping into the role of a leader, even if you're not confident. You can start by being a part of a small organization, joining a charity, or starting your own group. You can build up the leadership skills necessary through books, courses, mentorships, and coaching. Building up these traits and developing these skills takes time. Remember, you have the *F.O.R.C.E.*™ within you to take on the challenge in front of you. Develop both your natural and hidden strengths so you can lead by example by doing just *1% More* and becoming that extraordinary leader!

CHAPTER 38

THE POWER OF
ONE PERCENT!

Your beliefs become your thought; your thoughts become your words; your words become your actions; your actions become your habits: your habits become your values; your values become your destiny."

— *Unknown*

Wow! What a fantastic journey we have been on so far. I know the insights and inspirational stories you have heard from the authors have impacted your life on some deep emotional level. I know they have for me!

Looking back to the boy I once was: shy, insecure, overweight, and feeling not good enough. I am now coaching clients, facilitating seminars and workshops, hosting a podcast show, speaking on stage, and becoming a published author. This journey is quite surprising, even to me! I never imagined that my life would turn out this way. As my mother says, *"everything happens for a reason."* My reason is to be here, with you, on this exciting quest.

I want to be frank and vulnerable with you. My life has not been perfect in any way, and it is still challenged in various areas, but I haven't given up, and neither should you. If it wasn't for the events in my life, the people I've met, the hardship I've felt, and the experience I've gained, I would not be here with you currently. I would not have the knowledge and insight to share with you. I would not be able to give you the love and the strength you need to carry on. It has taken me years to do the work to offer forgiveness, release myself from the past, allow myself to happily fail, and allow me to love myself. I've recognized that there is still more to do as I constantly evolve and grow, and there will be more for you as well. If you feel a bit overwhelmed at the moment, please don't worry. Along with the coaches, leaders, and professionals within this book, I will continue to guide you; all you need is to take that first step and ask for assistance.

The power of *1 % More* has guided me throughout my life to give me the hope necessary to take the small actionable steps even when times looked bleak. It has helped me embrace the person I am today by giving me the strength to embrace another day.

I wish for this book to create a ripple effect of positive energy impacting everyone who reads it, both far and wide. I ask that you begin healing yourself from the pains of the past and focus on your actions today to build a better tomorrow. You have the power to create unlimited possibilities, so be accountable, take responsibility, and make your life extraordinary by doing that *1% More!*

Summary:

The One Percent More Path

We started this book by talking about the ***Extraordinary Being Movement's*** four core pillars of personal transformation. We said there are three things you need to do first. You need to develop your awareness, grow, and take action. Each of these leads to our fourth pillar and outcome, ***Impact.*** The impact is the effect caused by applying ***1% More*** to various aspects of your life, creating transformation for yourself and the world around you. As children, we were never taught clearly by our parents or by our education system to develop these four core pillars effectively.

Many of us have dabbled in the ideas and concepts, read a book, took a course but never entirely and whole-heartedly acted consistently and systematically to make it a part of our lives. As you can see by others' success and happiness, they have consciously decided to live life in this space.

Personal transformation takes time and effort to apply and be consistent daily. We only have so much time and energy, and that's why ***1% More*** allows you to add that little extra to our already busy lives.

In the first section of the book, we talked about ***Awareness*** and understanding where you are currently in life, how to discover what's working and what's not working, understanding knows and unknowns, finding opportunities through blind spots, and living with intention. We heard from our contributing writers on learning to be you, aligning your life, creating your purpose, living in wonder, and creating magic.

In the second section, **Growth**, we discussed the five growth areas, stretching outside the comfort zone living with integrity. Our authors shared planting those seeds of greatness, activating your life, understanding multi-dimensional reality, epiphany, the art of being you, growing beyond your limitations, partnerships, becoming a warrior, and creating your unique style.

In the third section, **Action**, we speak about being in action because nothing can be achieved without being in motion. We discussed creating a system that works for your lifestyle, leveling up your goals, and breaking bad habits. We dove further into stories on self-care, choosing happiness, revealing your inner rockstar, having that winner's mindset on and off the field, mastering the Zorro circle, enrolling others, and how success and failure are our choices.

And in the fourth section, we brought all three together as we transitioned to **Impact**. We expressed that your time is now to make a choice, to continue living the way you are, or start applying what you have learned to do that *1% More*. We explored the hidden force within and how to harness success through the power of *1% More!*

This model is the key; it is your personal pathway from being stuck and unhappy to developing yourself to a new higher consciousness and becoming the person you were born to be.

This book is only a starting point to get you moving. We have only touched the tip of the iceberg on all these core areas. There is so much to learn, to do, and to achieve. As you begin to grow and expand you may want to explore deeper into other aspects of personal development, which we highly encourage you to do.

Before you begin to continue your journey into the world of personal development, here are three things you should do...

#1 - Create a Plan

There are two types of plans you can create in your life right now. You can create a plan for failure or a plan for success. A plan for failure is loosely slapped together ideas of things you may want to do and explore but will never eventually do. A plan for success is stating your purpose, understanding your *"Why,"* setting clear and measurable goals, and focusing on being intentional towards your dream. A success plan is about what you need to do presently and, in the days ahead, to create a future for tomorrow. It's holding yourself responsible, accountable, and taking ownership of your life.

#2 - Be in Action!

Your time is now to choose, stay where you are, unhappy and unsatisfied with your life, or move forward and become fearless. Fear is a state of mind. It's a choice. To be fearless, you must remember that this situation is only a moment in time. It's a moment you created in your mind. The difference between fear and danger is that danger is real. So, ask yourself, *is this fear I'm facing or a dangerous situation?* The chances are you are facing a bit of internal fear. If it is inner fear, this would be an opportunity to understand better where it comes from.

At times, I reflect on my life and laugh. How can I be fearless and parachute out of a plane, possibly to my death, but find approaching someone I am attracted to more fearful? These fearful beliefs vary based upon the level of value we create for each circumstance. For me, jumping from a plane would be less scary than being rejected. Our belief system limits our abilities and the fearful thoughts we add to them.

Believe in yourself! Place yourself in action, be courageous and learn to love failure, become resilient and learn practical ways to recover when things go wrong. Develop a mindset for success; take control of your thoughts, perceptions, and intentions to gain the knowledge necessary to make better decisions by discovering what appropriate actions must be performed every day.

#3 - Hire a Coach!

If you want to take your journey to a whole new level, then hire a coach. I'm not saying that because I am one, I am saying that because I genuinely believe in the effectiveness of coaching. I have multiple coaches in various areas such as business, personal, and health. I have seen my performance and confidence increase time and time again. Having a coach allowed me to find my purpose, get clarity around my business and life, and help me harness the passion inside me to keep moving forward. I would not be writing this book today if it weren't for coaching! The best part of coaching is having someone in your corner who understands the process and will unconditionally support you every step of the way. They are there to lift you, hold you accountable, address your blind spots, and provide valuable insight.

Throughout this book, you have been gifted with the opportunity to meet many different coaches, each with their unique approach. Please take a moment, view their website, set up a one-to-one, and see who is the best fit for you. They are here to assist you in your growth and offer you opportunities for unlimited success!

The Extraordinary Being Movement Is Here To Serve You!

No matter what path you take, we are here to serve you! Through our podcast show, ongoing training, speaking events, and even our own coaching programs we want to make miracles happen in your life.

The only way to make that happen is if:

- You are ready to be coached.
- You are ready to stop dipping your toes in the water and dive in head-first.
- You are ready to dedicate your time and energy to yourself.
- You are ready to make a difference in the lives of others.
- You are ready to align your life and business.
- You are ready to commit to weekly calls and growth work.
- You are ready to clarify your vision.
- You are ready to try new ideas and move away from old ones.

If you are ready…

Then take action and visit our website at:
ExtraordinaryBeingMovement.com
or join us on ***Facebook***
and be a part of the transformational movement.

Please, spread the word about this book, the website, and our mission. We would love to meet you at a live event or program.

Schedule a one-to-one with us today to begin your journey in life. We will coach you through the four pillars of ***Awareness, Growth,*** and ***Action*** so you can make an ***Impact*** in your life.

I want to thank you again for being a part of this extraordinary journey with us. If there is anything I can ever do for you, please let me know. I wish you the best!

To Your Success!

Len DeCarmine

About The Author

*L*en DeCarmine coaches people to find their authentic selves and connect with their inner power to create and have the courage to gain the highest level of success.

He is the C.E.O. and co-founder of the Extraordinary Being Movement, a full-service personal development coaching company and podcast show. He has a passionate and holistic approach that allows people to stay grounded in the present moment. His personal experiences over 20 years have given him the skills necessary to help people break free of unhealthy patterns, thoughts, and behaviors to grow to their full potential.

He has studied and trained as a Certified Life and Business Coach, with an emphasis in Neuro-Linguistic Programming, Cognitive Behavior Therapy, and Mindfulness. Len has worked with individuals, groups, and businesses to help them achieve their goals, focusing on his four pillars of success; Awareness, Growth, Action, and Impact. He offers online courses, coaching, and retreats to help people learn how to live extraordinary lives.

AUTHOR CONTACT INFORMATION

Leonard D. DeCarmine, *Transformational Coach*
Website: ExtraordinaryBeingMovement.com
Email: len@extraordinarybeingmovement.com
Social: @ExtraordinaryBeingMovement (Facebook)
@Len DeCarmineCoach (Facebook)
@lendecarminecoach (IG)
@yourcoachlen (Twitter)
www.linkedin.com/in/lendecarmine

WE INVITE REVIEWS!

Please return to the online outlet that you purchased
this book from and post a review.

Thank you!